Widowhood: The Next Chapter

I'm Still Here - Now What?

Bobbie Bennett

Contents

The artistic illustration is created by Lilian Suzette Salcido.
"Just when the caterpillar thought the world was over, it became a butterfly."
Zhuang Zhou, Chinese philosopher, 4th Century BCE

Dedication

I dedicate this book to the memory of my sister, Rose, and my brother, Jimmy.
You will live forever in my heart.

Disclaimer

This book is intended for informational and educational purposes only and does not constitute legal advice. The information contained herein is not intended to create, and receipt of it does not constitute, an attorney-client relationship between the reader and the author or publisher.

Laws regarding death, inheritance, estate planning, and related matters are complex, subject to frequent change, and vary significantly by state, country, and jurisdiction. While every effort has been made to provide accurate and current information, the author and publisher make no representations or warranties of any kind, express or implied, about the completeness, accuracy, reliability, or suitability of the information contained in this book.

The author, publisher, and any affiliated parties shall not be liable for any loss, damage, or legal consequences arising directly or indirectly from the use of this book or reliance upon its contents. Readers assume full responsibility for any actions taken based on information in this book.

The information provided may not reflect the most current legal developments and should not be considered a substitute for consultation with qualified legal professionals. Laws change regularly, and legal outcomes depend on specific facts and circumstances unique to each situation.

We strongly recommend that readers consult with licensed attorneys in their jurisdiction before making any legal decisions or taking any actions related to estate planning, inheritance, or related legal matters.

By using this book, you acknowledge that you have read and understood this disclaimer and agree to its terms.

Contributors' stories have been included with permission, though some names and identifying details may have been changed to protect privacy.

Prologue

This isn't just another memoir. It's a survival guide wrapped in an unforgettable story. Bobbie's journey through three marriages, two funerals, and a divorce offers valuable insights on starting over. Her story shows that life's most devastating chapters can become its most powerful turning points.

Her first marriage pulled her into the shadowy world of organized crime, where she insisted that dinner guests check their firearms at the door. Bobbie recalls one night when Tony was away on "business," and a violent storm covered the area. Lightning wasn't the only thing that struck; a gunshot echoed through the thunder, and by dawn, Tony's prized quarter horse was found dead in its stall, shot execution-style between the eyes. At daybreak, the terrified ranch hand delivered the devastating news. The morning headlines told the story she'd been fearing.

Years later, after losing her first husband, Bobbie surprised everyone by falling deeply in love with Danny, a man ten years her junior who still got carded at restaurants. Their life was filled with ski trips, family vacations, and home parties without the worries of their friends needing a background check. Eventually, their marriage gradually unraveled when his wandering eye proved stronger than their wedding vows, leading to an inevitable but amicable parting of ways.

The core of the story centers on Bobbie's third husband and true soulmate. Clayton, the methodical engineer, fell in love with a free-spirited former go-go dancer and entertainer. While he was calibrating his 3D milling machines, she was memorizing lines for a stage role or a local television commercial. They were living proof that opposites don't just attract; they can create something extraordinary until death tore them apart.

But here's what makes this book revolutionary: it's not just Bobbie's story. There are also the voices of fellow survivors, widows, and widowers who share their raw, honest journeys through grief and into new beginnings. Their collective wisdom and diverse perspectives help guide others to find new paths.

The practical guidance addresses the questions that keep you awake at 3 AM:

• **To Date or Not to Date:** When your heart is ready, but your mind isn't sure

• **Eliminating Skeletons:** The emotional archaeology of cleaning out a shared life

• **Taking Care of Business:** Navigating the legal maze when you can barely navigate grief

This is more than a memoir; it's a masterclass in resilience. With unflinching honesty and unexpected humor, it reveals how life's most devastating endings can become your most powerful new beginnings. Whether you're facing loss, supporting someone who is, or simply wondering how people survive the unthinkable, this book will change how you see both heartbreak and hope with a touch of humor.

"Widowhood: The Next Chapter, I'm Still Here-Now What?" is a perfect gift for anyone ready to discover that starting over isn't just possible, it's where the best chapter begins.

For more information go to www.bobbiebennett.com

Chapter 1 - Part 1 - The First Husband

Three Wedding Rings – The First of Three Marriages

With this ring, I thee wed...

My first wedding ring was a simple gold band that fit loosely on my finger, often threatening to slip off during the most ordinary moments of my extraordinary life.

My new Italian husband, Tony, was connected to the Chicago mob. We met one fateful night when I was "Go-Go" dancing at a popular nightclub in the suburbs. Little did I know that while shaking my hips under the pulsing disco lights, I would catch the sharp eye of someone with connections more tangled than a plate of fettuccine.

My career as a Go-Go dancer was short-lived, thanks to Tony. Apparently, seeing me dance in that glass cage while other men and women looked at me like I was the last slice of pizza at a party was more than he could handle. So, I decided to hang up my Go-Go boots and dive into the world of live theater. Tony loved it! He thought watching me transform into various characters was hilarious, and I was happy just to be on stage.

Tony was the perfect gentleman during our dating period, always taking me to the most exclusive places in the Windy City. I swear we never needed a reservation. The moment he walked in, the hosts practically tripped over themselves to get us the best seats in the house. It felt a bit over the top. At one restaurant, the chef himself came out from the kitchen, wiping his hands on his apron, to shake Tony's hand and kiss both my cheeks. "It is my honor," he said with tears in his eyes, "my absolute honor to feed you tonight."

As thrilling as this was, I began to feel overwhelmed. I grew up on a poor farm in Southern Illinois, where the biggest crime was stealing corn from a neighbor's field. The more I learned about Tony's business, the more nervous I became. Just as I was about to tell him that we should take a step back in our relationship, he surprised me with a proposal. Before I knew it, we exchanged vows and committed to spending the rest of our lives together. A whirlwind moment marked the start of a new chapter in our lives. Tony's mom and dad, my brother, Joey, my sister, Maria, and her family, and some close friends attended the ceremony. However, my mom, who was living in Arizona, was unable to attend at the time, which left a little ache in my chest. I really needed her with me during this wonderful and terrifying time in my life.

After our spontaneous ceremony, my husband drove me straight to his mother Sofia's house. She lived in a charming Italian community called "The Old Neighborhood." Tony believed it would be beneficial for me to stay with his mom for a while so she could teach me the secrets of cooking the beloved Italian dishes he cherished throughout his life. It was a far cry from what I was used to on the farm. My childhood meals consisted of fried chicken, watermelon, and collard greens; you know, the kind of meals that made you feel like you needed a nap right afterward.

I spent the entire week with my mother-in-law, learning how to make her favorite dishes, including her famous Sunday gravy, which she insists is the secret sauce to making any Italian meal taste amazing. Even though her English was limited because of her strong Italian accent, we bonded over laughter as we both cooked different meals made with love. It's one of my favorite memories of her. I feel so lucky to have had the chance to learn from one of the most respected cooks in the Old Neighborhood.

By the end of the week, my husband and his family gathered for Sunday dinner. Sofia announced, "I no cook nothing. Everything you eat, my new daughter, she make it." Everyone's expression shifted to blank stares. I stood in the warmth of the kitchen, watching my new family gather around the dining table, their plates filled with an assortment of their favorite Italian dishes. The rich aroma of chicken cacciatore filled the air, with tender pieces of chicken simmered perfectly in a savory tomato sauce. Next to it were slices of eggplant parmesan, golden and bubbling, a perfect mix of crispy breadcrumbs and creamy cheese. Giant stuffed shells overflowed with a rich mixture of ricotta and spinach, while Italian meatballs were seasoned flawlessly. For dessert, I made a homemade cheesecake, its velvety texture and subtle sweetness sure to delight.

Yet, amid the clinking of forks and the sounds of satisfied laughter, the most heartwarming sight was my husband's expression. After the last bite had disappeared and the table was cleared, he turned to me with his captivating smile, his eyes shining with affection. "Now I can take my wife home!" he declared, his voice full of pride and joy, making my heart swell with happiness.

To this day, I can still feel the warmth of that kitchen and see the joy on my husband's face. Cooking became my love language, my way of showing care when words weren't enough. Every dinner party, every family gathering, every quiet meal was an opportunity to see that same expression of pure contentment cross someone's face. Because sometimes, the most beautiful moments in life happen around a table full of food made with love.

Our marriage felt like a thrilling rollercoaster ride, full of unexpected twists and turns. Tony and I got along well as long as I played the role of the oblivious partner. After all, does a woman really need to know where her husband disappears to during odd hours of the night? He could be out saving puppies or sitting in a van on an all-night stakeout. My closet started to resemble a fashion show, thanks to all the Oleg Cassini and Pierre Cardin outfits he kept bringing home for me to wear. And let's not forget the jewelry; I never imagined I would need a safe to lock away so much gold.

As exciting as everything sounded, I wasn't truly happy. What I needed was to see my mom. She had retired to Phoenix, Arizona, a few years earlier, and I wanted to confide in her about my new married life. I was seeking sound advice, and I knew she would give it. When I told Tony that I wanted to spend time with my mom, he bought plane tickets for me, himself, my nineteen-year-old brother,

Joey, and my sister's two boys, Michael and Mark. He said my mom would be thrilled to see her son and two grandsons, and he was definitely right.

As we landed in Phoenix in late August, the scorching desert air wrapped around us warmly. I saw my mom eagerly waiting for us, her excitement visible as she looked forward to meeting her new son-in-law. They hugged, and with a playful yet serious smile, she warned him to take good care of me, or he'd have to deal with her! Then Mom hugged her two grandsons, showering them with love. Her smile grew tearful when she finally saw her son Joey; it was obvious she missed him deeply. They were all ready for a week of adventure with her, so she picked up the boys and told me we would reconnect later.

Tony and I rented a car and drove to our luxurious hotel in Scottsdale, where the shimmering pools and Southwestern architecture promised a delightful stay. Tony's aunt Eileen had recently moved to Phoenix from Chicago with her family, and he was eager to visit them as soon as we unpacked. I decided to stay behind and relax by the pool, where I could get that perfect vacation tan. When he left, I eagerly slipped into my bathing suit and headed to the inviting pool, ready to bask in the sunshine and enjoy some "me time" in the desert atmosphere.

I learned a painful lesson about the unforgiving nature of the Arizona summer sun and how it affects my fair skin. After just a few hours of exposure, I was left with angry, red blisters all over my body. Moving hurt. Breathing hurt. Being alive hurt.

I was crying in our room when Tony walked in. He helped me soak in the soothing, cool waters of the bathtub as we waited for the house doctor to arrive. But as soon as my mom saw me, she rushed outside and came back with a peculiar-looking plant with long, prickly green stems. I later discovered that it was an aloe vera plant that grows wild in the desert.

When the doctor finally arrived, he inspected my burns and thanked my mom for treating them with the best remedy available, recognizing the healing properties of aloe vera. At that moment, I felt a wave of gratitude and pride for my mom's knowledge of natural medicine. She always found a way to bring me comfort.

While my husband bonded with his aunt and her family, I embraced my new role as a professional bed lounger and took my status as a recovering burn victim very seriously. With the soft, cool hotel sheets wrapped around me like a royal robe, I discovered the unexpected joy of daytime television. The Rita Davenport Show caught my attention with her soothing southern drawl that took me back to my farm days, and her sense of humor was just what I needed. I tuned into her show on KPHO (channel 5) every morning until the day we left. I surrendered to the fact that if I wanted a golden glow in the future, I would indulge in a spray tan.

I intentionally postponed our complicated mother-daughter conversation while my mom was immersed in heartfelt moments with her son and grandkids, creating memories that would become cherished family treasures. I needed time not only to heal from the so-called Arizona vacation but also to reconsider my doubts about my marriage.

After we returned home from the desert, we noticed the streets seemed dirtier than before, and traffic was much more congested. Winter greeted us with a record-breaking snowstorm that shut down the entire city. After some serious discussions, my brother Joey, Tony, and I made our first big decision: we are moving to sunny Arizona!

We were all excited about living in Scottsdale. Without Tony's goombah friends around, he finally had the chance to lead a more normal life. Everything seemed perfect until tragedy struck.

The haunting sound of sirens pierced the evening air while I was performing in a community theater production on the Scottsdale stage, just a stone's throw from the hospital. In that moment, a wave of uncertainty washed over me. As my fellow cast members and I exchanged worried glances, we felt the weight of concern for the real world right outside the door, disrupting the theatrical experience we were trying to create inside.

Joey, my rock, my best friend, and my dear brother, was taken from me in an instant, leaving behind a void that felt impossible to fill. He was simply walking along McDowell Road, which at that time was just a dirt path, when a drunk driver tragically struck him down, ending his life without warning. The shock of his loss shattered my world, and I found myself engulfed in profound grief that seemed to consume every part of me.

During this dark time, Tony was a beacon of support, tirelessly trying to bring me comfort. His kindness and patience never wavered, even as I struggled to open up, weighed down by my sorrow. In an effort to help me heal, he took me on day trips through the stunning landscapes of Arizona, hoping to remind me of the beauty still present in the world. We explored the majestic red rock formations near Sedona and admired the snow-capped peak of Flagstaff as we navigated the untouched expanses of the Sonoran Desert. Yet, despite the breathtaking sights around me, I felt numb; the beauty seemed to glide past me without making a connection.

As my appetite vanished and I began to feel frail and empty, I longed to retreat to Joey's room, seeking solace in silence and the embrace of my memories. I drowned in my thoughts and emotions, trying to process the unbearable loss. No matter how heavy my heart felt, Tony continued to stand by me, patiently waiting for the moment when I might glimpse a flicker of hope in the depths of my despair.

How could I imagine life without him, especially after the deep bond we forged as children? When our parents divorced, my brother, sister, and I were very young. The situation quickly became chaotic; each parent took us to separate grandparents' homes while custody was being determined. Eventually, the court granted my father custody of my older sister, Marie, while Joey and I stayed with our mother. Shortly after the custody arrangement, our mother placed us with her parents on their farm in southern Illinois while she worked in Chicago to save enough money for a home we could call our own in the city.

Though our grandparents cared for us, they were overwhelmed by the demanding tasks of farm life, tending to the crops, caring for animals, and managing endless daily chores. Having Joey beside me was my comfort during this unsettling time. As our grandparents focused on maintaining the farm, I naturally stepped into the role of looking after both of us. I made sure Joey ate well, had clean clothes, and felt loved, doing my best to create the stability and warmth we both needed during this challenging chapter of our childhood.

One day, not long after Joey's death, while driving north on Invergordon Road in Paradise Valley, I almost had a terrible accident. Swerving over a ditch beside the road to avoid hitting another vehicle sent my car airborne before it crashed into a telephone pole, splitting it in half. The top half, still attached to the wires, swung back and pierced through the windshield, missing decapitating me by mere inches. Surviving unscathed led to an epiphany: if Joey needed me to join him on the other side, my life would have ended there. At that moment, I realized I had to pick up the pieces and move on. When our son was born two years later, I proudly named him Joey in honor of my brother.

We purchased a charming ranch-style home in North Scottsdale on a spacious acre of land. The property featured a rustic horse stable and an assortment of riding gear. Tony insisted that we fill the stable with a few riding horses, as we had decided to embrace our new Southwestern lifestyle. Inside, the home was decorated with rustic elegance and the charm of the Wild West.

Tony was meticulous about his home and clothes. When we first moved to Arizona, he transformed his wardrobe from a city slicker into an Italian Western cowboy. He owned two ten-gallon hats and several pairs of handmade leather boots. I swear, Tony had more clothes than most men, and even more than many women I knew. I occupied a quarter of our closet while the rest overflowed with his Western wear and leisure suits.

After settling into our new home, we boldly opened an Italian restaurant in Phoenix. The menu featured daily Italian specials along with delicious beef and sausage sandwiches. However, my "gravy" (spaghetti sauce) became the most popular among our customers, leading to a thriving demand for it; we sold it by the pint, quart, and half gallon. I spent all my time in the kitchen, preparing the daily specials and, of course, the gravy. We had dedicated employees to help with all the other positions needed to run a successful business. Tony was the perfect front of the house Maitre D'.

After a year, the demanding work and long hours took a toll on my health and our marriage. I found myself losing weight and constantly feeling fatigued. I worked tirelessly, always in the kitchen, and rarely had a day off. I felt like an automaton, simply going through the motions. This was not how I envisioned my life.

Tony started taking money from the till every day and rushing to the track to place bets. His gambling habits escalated, leading me to confront him about it. One fateful day, my emotions boiled over. In a fit of rage, I grabbed a heavy cast-iron skillet from the kitchen and hurled it in his direction, narrowly missing his head. The look on his face was one of shock and fear. He had never seen that side of me before. In fact, I had never seen that side of me either!

While Tony resembled the Italian Stallion who had just stepped off a magazine cover, I glanced in the mirror and wondered who the ghost staring back at me was. I felt like a wrung-out dishrag left to dry.

Thus came our second big decision: sell the business or get a divorce. Naturally, we chose the option that didn't involve lawyers and awkward holiday dinners, so we sold the business. A year later, I discovered I was pregnant. We took a break from the stress and created a tiny human instead! What tremendous joy little Joey brought into our lives! His infectious laughter and playful spirit filled my world with warmth and happiness, creating memories I will cherish forever.

Tony wanted our son to be the best young horseback rider in town, so he purchased a striking Pinto pony named Canon. At first, I was happy to see them spend time together and bond as father and son. However, my joy quickly turned to anxiety as I watched little Joey get bucked off the spirited pony one too many times. Each time he hit the ground, Tony would lift him back up, insisting he try again. This approach was not acceptable for a five-year-old trying to prove his love for his father. Concerned for Joey's well-being and recognizing the risks involved in the frequent falls, I decided to take action. I donated Canon to Joey's Montessori School, which had a program that allowed children to learn about and care for live farm animals, ensuring both safety and educational opportunities for kids like Joey.

A few years later, Tony made headlines in the local newspaper with a sensational article titled "Chicago Mafia Comes to Phoenix." Soon after its publication, several concerned parents at our son's grade school expressed their worries. Their fears about their children befriending someone with family ties to organized crime became evident, creating an uncomfortable and tense atmosphere during school events. Faced with rising pressure and the troubling implications of Tony's notoriety, I enrolled our son in a private school where he could have better opportunities to learn without being overshadowed by his father's shady past.

Then came the night that changed everything. Tony was out of town on a business trip. A terrible storm struck our area with lightning bolts and thunder so loud that I didn't hear the gunshot that rang out from the stable.

At dawn, our ranch hand knocked on the back door. I could see the fear in his eyes that something was terribly wrong. The devastating news quickly made its way into our local newspapers. There, on the front page, was a photo of Tony's prize quarter horse lying in its stall, shot between the eyes.

As I stared at that awful photo, my mind went straight to The Godfather movie. I remembered the scene where the movie producer wakes up to find his prized racehorse's head in his bed. It turned out to be a bloody message from the mob. Tony's horse wasn't in our bedroom, but the message was just as clear. Someone wanted to send Tony a warning, and they were willing to kill something he loved to do it. The only difference was that in the movie, it was fiction. This was my real life, and I was terrified of what might come next.

Before long, the FBI tapped our phones, and I felt like someone was following me every time I left the house. Anxious and paranoid, I was reaching the end of my rope, unsure how much more I could take.

When Tony collapsed from that sudden, crushing heart attack, his death shocked everyone around me. However, something unexpected happened in that moment, a strange calm settled over my mind. I felt no overwhelming grief, no deep sadness, and no sense of devastating loss. After so many years of living on edge, always wondering what new danger might find us, his passing felt more like the end of a long, dark nightmare than a tragedy.

For the first time in years, I could breathe. I could imagine a second chance, a real opportunity to raise my son in peace, without fear lurking around every corner. The heavy weight of constant worry began to lift from my shoulders, replaced by something I hadn't felt in so long: hope.

While little Joey and I sat in our seats on that American Airlines flight from Phoenix to Chicago, I stared out the small window, watching the endless blue sky and puffy white clouds drift by. I tried to find comfort in the view. Flying usually made me feel free, but not this time. This time, I knew that beneath my feet, in the cold cargo hold below, lay a special casket carrying my husband's body home.

The funeral director in Chicago handled all the arrangements with care, ensuring that Tony would arrive with dignity. Choosing the funeral home wasn't difficult; most Italians from the Old Neighborhood ended up at the same place. But making that phone call to my mother-in-law, Nonna Sofia, to tell her that her oldest son was gone was one of the hardest things I'd ever had to do. Although she never admitted it, everyone knew that Tony was her favorite.

Joey and I stayed with Sofia during those heavy days in Chicago. Her small house was like a museum of memories. Every room filled with old family photos and treasures from Italy. At night, when the grief felt too heavy to bear alone, she would tell me stories about her childhood in the Old Country.

"Food, it was everything," she'd say, her weathered hands moving as if she were still kneading dough. "It brought together la famiglia (the family), you understand? From when I was piccola (small) so small, I learned the secret recipes my mama, she teach me, and her mama before that." When she came to America, she was determined to keep alive these traditions, to fill her new home with the same warmth and amore (love) that food had brought to her childhood in the old country.

I understood that sharing these stories was how she tried to heal her broken heart. I felt grateful to hear them, especially knowing that just one year later, Sofia would be gone too.

After losing Tony, I threw myself into building a new life for my son. I found a good job at a beautiful resort in Scottsdale. With my mother living close by, I never had to worry about leaving Joey with strangers. Those two had a special connection that lasted until the day she died.

Selling everything, the big house, the horses, and Tony's fancy Cadillac should have felt sad. But it didn't. As I packed up our things and moved us into a smaller, cozier home, I didn't feel like I was losing anything. Instead, it felt like I was finally free. The heavy burden I'd carried for so long was gone, and for the first time in years, I could see a bright future ahead for me and my son.

We were starting over, and it felt like coming alive again.

My sister Marie and her family moved from Chicago to Arizona to be closer to me and our mom. Marie truly loved Arizona. She was passionate about the great outdoors and often took my son and her two boys on exciting camping trips. They slept under the stars in the Grand Canyon and enjoyed thrilling rafting adventures down the Colorado River. Some of little Joey's best summer vacations were spent with his aunt and cousins.

My life as a single mom had begun, and although I hadn't planned this path, I found myself standing taller without the weight of Tony's world on my shoulders. Family, fun, and adventure surrounded my son to help fill the void left by his father's absence. As I gently placed my gold wedding band into a small velvet box and tucked it away, I realized this was merely the first chapter of my story-- the first of three rings that would mark the profound stages of my life's journey.

Chapter 1 - Part 2 - The Second Husband

Three Wedding Rings – The second of three marriages

For better or worse...

My second wedding ring was a stunning piece of jewelry: a wide gold band adorned with four dazzling diamonds. However, it felt loose on my finger and kept spinning around. I had it adjusted twice, but it stubbornly refused to stay in place, perhaps an early warning sign I chose to ignore.

Danny and I met while working at a luxurious five-star resort in North Scottsdale, nestled between the majestic Camelback Mountain and the slopes of Mummy Mountain. This enchanting locale felt less like a workplace and more like an extravagant playground, where the air was filled with the scent of blooming desert flowers and the gentle rustle of palm trees.

Danny, a decade younger than I, had an infectious smile that could brighten even the darkest days. I'll never forget the shock and disbelief that washed over his face when I finally revealed the identity of my first husband.

My life was a tapestry woven with secrets, stories, and truths I had carefully hidden away, never meant to see the light of day; Danny sensed this unspoken tension. He understood, without needing to pry, that some things were better left alone, untouched. Surprisingly, he didn't pull away or get upset when he found out. Instead, he wrapped his arms around me and told me it was time to let go of the past and focus on the future for little Joey and me. He was the kind of person who listened intently and offered a shoulder to lean on whenever I needed to vent. Danny was irresistible with his laid-back demeanor and delightful sense of humor, drawing me in with his charm and warmth.

As my relationship with Danny blossomed, my life turned into laughter and joy. He had an incredible talent for crafting spontaneous adventures for Joey and me, and this change was exactly what we both needed. For the first time in a long while, I no longer felt like a secret agent was following me or that my phone conversations were being monitored.

I felt excited and hopeful as I began a new journey of love and commitment. Our enchanting outdoor wedding ceremony took place on the resort's impeccably manicured grounds, surrounded by the stunning beauty of the Southwest. We exchanged our vows as the sun dipped low in the sky, casting a golden glow over Camelback Mountain. This backdrop made our special day even more magical.

My wedding dress was a soft powder blue, crafted from luxurious satin that shimmered gently in the light. My son was the perfect ring bearer, looking incredibly dapper in his dark blue suit. My sister, Marie, was the most beautiful maid of honor, and her elegance and beauty captivated everyone present. My hair stylist, Trudy, worked her magic on my sister after she was satisfied with my wedding hairstyle. Standing beside my handsome husband, I felt like the luckiest person in the world.

We embarked on our new journey by finding the perfect family home, which felt like a dream come true. The house featured an expansive, Olympic-sized pool, ideal for hosting memorable parties. I organized fun birthday events for little Joey without worrying that his friends would be unable to attend due to his late father's reputation.

Danny, the adventurer, surprised us by purchasing a sleek boat and took it upon himself to teach Joey and me how to water ski. In the winter, he arranged trips to beautiful mountain ski resorts, where my son and I experienced the thrill of snow skiing. Our family cherished our annual adventures to the magical realms of Disneyland and Universal Studios, where dreams really do come alive. Despite our busy schedules, Danny always made time for us, taking me on romantic getaways. Those intimate escapes were filled with treasured memories.

I felt happy and content with my life. When Danny suggested that we expand our family by having another child, I agreed. I wasn't surprised when I experienced a miscarriage; I was already thirty-nine years old, and it had been thirteen years since the birth of my son. The doctor assured us that we still had a chance if we tried again. We followed his advice, and just a month before I celebrated my 40th birthday, our beautiful and healthy daughter, Mia, entered the world. With her tiny fingers grasping my hand and her bright eyes taking in her new surroundings, she filled our hearts with indescribable joy. Danny was overwhelmed with pride and happiness as he held that precious bundle of joy.

Caution: When life appears too good to be true, it usually is.

When our sweet baby girl was shy of turning three, I received an unsettling phone call that would change my life. It was a co-worker from Danny's job, her voice shaky yet urgent as she insisted on sharing something troubling. She informed me that my husband was having an affair. Skepticism washed over me; I initially dismissed it as the ramblings of a disgruntled employee looking for revenge after being fired. I hung up, brushing off her words and hoping they were simply the product of someone's bitterness.

A few days later, I received another jolt from a different call, this time from a woman whose tone was markedly different from the first. Her voice was direct and self-assured. She confessed that she had been involved with my husband. As I listened, a whirlwind of emotions swirled within me: disbelief, anger, and intense curiosity. Ultimately, I agreed to meet her, eager to uncover the truth behind her confession and its implications for my family.

As two mature adults, we arranged to meet at a specific time in the afternoon at a public place to discuss this significant, life-altering situation. I was surprised to see a striking redhead in a business suit gesturing for me to join her at a corner booth in the back of the restaurant. Early in our conversation, I realized she believed my marriage to Danny was over. I stayed composed as she shared the details of their intimate love affair. When she handed me several photos of my husband lying stark naked on a couch with a rather large erection, I couldn't help but laugh. This brought a perplexed expression to Miss Redhead's face. I must confess I was also puzzled by my reaction.

After regaining my composure, I tucked the incriminating evidence into my purse, looked her straight in the eye, and said, "Sometimes we can be swept off our feet by handsome men who take our breath away. But don't confuse lust with love. My husband and I are very happy and do not plan to divorce. I'm sorry if you fell for a man who was acting out sexual fantasies with you, but that's all it was. He loves his family, and I won't let this one mistake of infidelity ruin our future together. With your beauty and integrity, I'm sure you'll have no trouble finding the man of your dreams. It's just not my man. You need to move on." With that, I walked away.

After I confronted my husband about the nude pictures and discussed the advice I had given to his red-haired playmate, he apologized profusely and assured me it wouldn't happen again. Ignoring my mother's warning, I gave him another chance to be a faithful husband and devoted father.

To reignite his attraction to me, I dyed my hair red, thinking it would catch his eye. Looking back, I realize that was misguided in many ways, but when a woman feels scorned, she can act unpredictably. I remained a redhead for a few months before returning to my blonde color.

We had convinced ourselves that Danny's extramarital lover had finally faded from our lives, but fate had one last dramatic *Fatal Attraction* moment in store for us. After an enjoyable evening at a dinner party, we returned home feeling relaxed and tired.

Danny was in the shower when I heard a strange sound coming from the roof. Intrigued yet slightly uneasy, I cautiously opened the front door and peered into the dim night, half-expecting to see a raccoon rummaging through our trash. Instead, illuminated by the soft glow of the porch light, I saw a shadowy figure lurking in the darkness, tossing pebbles onto our roof.

My heart began to race furiously as I recognized the unmistakable silhouette; it was her, that unpredictable redhead who seemed utterly obsessed with my husband. I swear, her throws could rival those of a toddler at a baseball game; one pebble landed with a thud while another sailed straight over the house.

In a surge of protective instinct that I can only describe as a superhero mindset, I called out to our two powerful Shar-Peis. The night air filled with the sound of their nails clicking frantically against the tile floor as they rushed to my side, their sleek muscles shifting beneath their thick, wrinkled skin. With my heart pounding in my ears, I opened the door wider and let them burst into the night. Sensing my distress, the dogs launched forward like furry torpedoes.

The intruder, her eyes wide with panic and caught off guard by the ferocious duo, scrambled back to her car. A moment later, she was gone, tires screeching against the asphalt as she sped into the darkness, leaving a thick haze of tension in the air.

Shortly after our experience with the *Fatal Attraction* encounter, Danny suggested that it might be the right time to accept a job offer in Palm Springs, California. I wholeheartedly agreed, feeling that a change of scenery could be just what we needed.

We found a responsible couple to rent our home in Cave Creek for the next year. Understanding that this move was temporary, Joey was willing to transfer to a school in Palm Desert, knowing that Danny and I were committed to a fresh start in rebuilding our relationship.

It's interesting how easily I can embrace change. Setting a specific timeframe for my commitments makes the process much smoother and more manageable. Moving to California was an adjustment for the entire family. Joey, a junior in high school, found this transition particularly challenging. Making new friends at that age isn't always easy. However, he always wanted the best for me and understood that I was working hard to make my marriage work. So, he agreed to do whatever it took to make me happy.

Our daughter Mia and her nanny, Chuyita, quickly adapted to our new home, a charming duplex in Palm Desert. The highlight of our property was the vast backyard with lush green grass. This expansive green space, free from fences, invited a sense of community among the homes on our block, all of which shared this lovely outdoor sanctuary. At the heart of the backyard lay a sparkling community pool, a vibrant hub of daily activity. A lively group of children welcomed Mia, always eager to play. One of the moms introduced us to the exciting world of pageantry. When Mia saw her new best friend practicing for a local pageant, she begged us to let her audition.

Mia's favorite movie was *The Wizard of Oz*. She watched it so often that she could recite Dorothy's lines before they left the character's lips. It was only fitting that when it came time for her debut on stage at her first pageant, she chose to tell the enchanting story of *The Wizard of Oz*. With her heart full of excitement and a sparkle in her eyes, she brought the magical tale to life, capturing the wonder and adventure that resonated with her so deeply. I shed proud tears when she won first place as Little Miss Palm Springs! Her prize included an all-expense-paid trip to the Beverly Hills Hotel in Los Angeles and four tickets to Disneyland. Additionally, she was entered in the National Tiny Miss America Pageant.

The national pageant was out of her league. Most of those kids had agents and coaches and had been performing since they could walk. Still, I didn't want to disappoint my daughter, so off we went to Beverly Hills. I'll never forget watching my little girl walk up to that microphone, eager to share her story about Dorothy and her friends. She practically glowed with excitement. Before the emcee even finished his introduction, she was already telling her tale, her voice bright and enthusiastic. Then it happened. The emcee's voice boomed across the vast auditorium, sharp and cold, cutting her off mid-sentence. "Hold on a minute", he said, "nobody upstages the emcee." The scolding was so harsh and public that I watched my confident little girl shrink before my eyes. The sparkle disappeared from her face as the color drained away, leaving her looking small and lost under those bright lights.

"Mom, where are you?" she whispered into the microphone, her voice breaking just a little. My heart shattered. There I was, sitting in that dark audience, completely helpless while my baby searched for me. All I wanted was to rush onto that stage, scoop her up, and tell her she was perfect just as she was. I couldn't shake the guilt that washed over me; I was the one who had placed this burden on her at such a tender age.

Mia finished her story, skimming through the key parts to reach the end. She was braver than I would have been. She recovered from the experience much quicker than I did, which I believed indicated the end of her beauty pageants.

When we moved back to our home in Cave Creek, Arizona, two years later, our busy lives continued on. Danny thrived in his career, Joey began his college journey, Mia attended the local charter school and took part in numerous community theater productions, and I managed a western gift shop in town. For several years, we settled into what felt like domestic contentment. Joey graduated from college, Mia continued to flourish, and Danny and I led our busy, parallel lives. But beneath the surface, something was changing.

My second marriage lasted, for the most part, seventeen wonderful years. As the ten-year age gap between us became more noticeable, I couldn't help but think that Danny would one day look at me and wonder how he went from marrying an exciting, mature woman to a vintage classic. Each new line on my face widened the invisible distance between us. Who knew love could come with an expiration date? I found myself both resenting and understanding the inevitable shift as our age difference became more apparent with each passing year.

When I discovered he was seeing a younger woman, it felt like déjà vu all over again. A decade had passed since I first confronted his infidelity, and now history was repeating itself—only with more shared memories and entangled lives at stake. The realization hit hard, leaving me feeling betrayed and exhausted. This time, it wasn't just my heart breaking; it was watching our family life crumble. The home we had built, the routines we had established, and the inside jokes we had shared over seventeen years suddenly felt like a beautiful sandcastle with the tide rushing in. I could no longer find the strength or desire to pull him back into the life we had built together. I knew it was time to face the painful truth: I had to let him go, accepting that sometimes love means setting someone free when they long for a different life.

Dealing with divorce was more challenging for me than coping with the death of my first husband. When a spouse passes away, it signifies a permanent loss; you won't see them at gatherings or family events. In contrast, with divorce, especially when children are involved, it becomes crucial to maintain a different kind of relationship. Fortunately, my second husband and I experienced an amicable and private divorce. We sold our home, split the proceeds, and divided our time with Mia.

I never expected to be separated from our mutual friends or to stop spending time with my ex's family, particularly my ex-mother-in-law. I tried to maintain our relationship by visiting her weekly for meaningful conversations. We shared a special bond that I didn't want to lose. She had become not just family but also a friend and confidant. However, after a few months, I realized it wasn't fair to

Danny's new girlfriend, who was trying to integrate into the family. As a result, I gradually distanced myself from their lives altogether.

When I found myself surrounded by a cloud of depression, I bravely chose to seek professional counseling. The experience was life-changing. Through several sessions, I gradually gave myself the precious gift of self-love and appreciation. I uncovered the beauty in my unique qualities and recognized my many positive contributions to the world around me. With this renewed perspective, I shifted my focus to my needs and those of my family, creating a nurturing environment for all of us. I often stood in front of the mirror and confidently declared, "This is my life, and I have the power to set my own rules!"

Embracing this epiphany, I envisioned a vibrant future, rich with possibilities and new beginnings ready to unfold. I placed my second wedding ring, that beautiful yet perpetually loose band, in the same velvet box as the first, a collection of lessons rather than failures. Each ring had shaped me, taught me, and ultimately freed me to become more authentically myself. Little did I know that the universe was already preparing to place a third ring on my finger that would fit perfectly.

Chapter 1 - Part 3 - The Third Husband

Three Wedding Rings – The third of three marriages

Till death do us part

My third wedding ring arrived as a surprise and fit perfectly, as if it had been waiting for my finger all along. Third time's a charm, as they say, and in my case, the old adage proved remarkably accurate.

After my divorce from Danny, I invested my share of the proceeds from selling our house to buy a new home in Cave Creek, Arizona. With my daughter, Mia, just a year away from graduating eighth grade, I wanted her to remain in the same school district. Meanwhile, my son, Joey, lived in a dorm at ASU.

I managed a bustling, Western-style gift shop in Frontier Town that attracted tourists from around the globe. Our shelves overflowed with handmade treasures from various Indigenous tribes. We offered turquoise and silver jewelry, cozy blankets, and hand-woven rugs featuring patterns that tell unique stories. We showcased a wide array of distinctive souvenirs that captured the essence of the area, along with a selection of clothing in vibrant colors. A tour bus arrived every day, filled with enthusiastic visitors eager to enjoy a hearty traditional BBQ feast served in the rustic old West restaurant next door. Before embarking on their next western adventure, tourists would wander into my shop to buy that must-have authentic dreamcatcher or turquoise jewelry to take home and share their journey with friends and family.

Between juggling my daughter's multiple school plays, dance recitals, and the demands of running a successful business, dating was the last thing on my mind. However, my sister, Marie, wanted to set me up with one of her co-workers, who she believed I would have much in common with. He had been married twice: one marriage ended in divorce, and the other concluded with the death of his spouse. I was curious since we both had similar experiences in marriage, so I finally agreed to let her give this mystery man my number.

I still remember the phone call I received that Sunday morning from a man with the sexiest voice I'd ever heard. His name was Clayton. He began the conversation by saying he wanted to take his tiger out that afternoon and wondered if I would like to join him. Uncertain about the reference to his tiger, yet intrigued by the seductive innuendo, I sputtered, "Wait a minute, just who do you think you're talking to? I'm not interested in seeing your, ahem... tiger!" There was a moment of confused silence before he stammered, 'My tiger... a classic British sports car... such a beautiful day for a drive... I just thought.' Poor guy, I had him flustered while I sat there wondering if I should be embarrassed or amused by my own gutter mind. Clearly, I had watched too many episodes of "Desperate Housewives."

I was instantly captivated when I saw this charming silver-haired man sitting behind the wheel of his stunning 1965 cobalt blue Sunbeam Tiger convertible. He wore a soft black Italian leather jacket, and his dazzling smile stirred something deep within me. His brilliant Paul Newman blue eyes mesmerized me, and I felt compelled to learn more about him. (I also felt compelled to check if my lipstick was still on straight, but that's beside the point.)

I knew he was my kind of guy when he whisked me away to the legendary Western watering hole in North Scottsdale, Greasewood Flats. Now, I'll admit I was expecting dinner at a nice restaurant, not a place that looked like it might blow away in the next dust storm. But sometimes the best surprises come in the most unexpected packages – kind of like finding a diamond ring in a Cracker Jack box.

This gritty bunkhouse-turned-saloon and restaurant was packed with bikers, cowboys, and locals every weekend. Clayton parked his stunning sports car next to a line of motorcycles in the dusty parking lot, and I couldn't help but giggle at the sight. It was like parking a tuxedo next to a row of overalls – both perfectly fine, just hilariously different.

We cleared a space at one of the rustic outdoor picnic tables littered with empty beer bottles. I tried to look graceful while brushing off suspicious crumbs and what I hoped was just dried ketchup. We ordered a couple of burgers, and I silently thanked the dating gods that I'd worn jeans instead of my fancy dress.

The afternoon flew by, and I was surprised at how comfortable I felt sharing stories from my past. It was the first time since my divorce that I had laughed so much at someone else's wit and humor – and not just nervous laughter, but the real, belly-shaking kind that makes your cheeks hurt.

A cowboy singer strummed his guitar, serenading us with nostalgic tunes that captured the spirit of the Old West. His voice was about as smooth as sandpaper, but somehow it added to the charm. Couples twirled and danced across the dirt floor, kicking up little clouds of dust with each step.

Inside the shack, the walls and ceiling were covered with hundreds of dollar bills, all signed and dated by the eclectic patrons who wandered in. I wondered how many of those bills represented someone's grocery money that got sacrificed to become part of the décor. It was like the world's most expensive wallpaper. It became evident to me that an exciting world existed that I wanted to be part of.

But you know what? Sometimes the best adventures start in the most unlikely places. And sometimes the man of your dreams drives up in a fancy sports car and takes you to eat burgers with bikers. Life has a funny way of surprising you when you least expect it.

After several months of dating, Clayton surprised me with an exciting invitation to a five-day adventure at a Sunbeam Tiger car rally in California. I was thrilled at the thought since I had never experienced the exhilaration of a car rally before.

When we arrived at the iconic Queen Mary in Long Beach, California, I was captivated by the sight of thirty-two gleaming Sunbeam Tiger sports cars. Each car showcased a remarkable blend of vintage charm and power, coming from different parts of the country.

The air was filled with excitement as we caravanned along the stunning Pacific Coast Highway. Clayton looked incredibly handsome behind the wheel of that sleek blue convertible. His strength and confidence radiated as he skillfully navigated the curves of the coastal highway. The engine purred with a sense of power, and combined with his effortless charm, it created a magnetic aura that continually drew my gaze back to him. The drive was truly spectacular, with the sun shimmering on the ocean to one side while the cliffs rose majestically on the other.

Our journey took us to the charming town of Eureka, just north of San Francisco. Surrounded by the town's Victorian architecture, Clayton took my hand and proposed, making the trip unforgettable. I had no idea that the whole rally team knew of Clayton's plans when we arrived at our destination. The sudden seriousness of our relationship genuinely took me aback. Although I liked him a lot and we had such a great time together, I wasn't in love with him and told him so. He could only respond, "You will learn to love me if you give me a chance." Those piercing bright blue eyes revealed something genuine, and he repeated, "Just give me a chance." So, I decided to do just that.

Clayton and I envisioned the ideal setting for our wedding on the deck of his cabin in Beaver Valley. Even though it was still a work in progress, the plywood floors and bare drywall created a uniquely inviting atmosphere. Our guests smiled at the unfinished surroundings, which included folding tables and chairs. The ceremony took place on the side deck with Little Diamond Rim Mountain as our backdrop. Surrounded by our loving family and neighbors from Beaver Valley, it was November 1, 1997, and the weather was perfect. I could hear the faint murmur of the East Verde River drifting through the crisp air.

I remain grateful to this day, simply knowing in my heart that the Lord allowed me to believe in Clayton. When we decided to sell our homes to buy our "forever home," we discovered we both had the same dream: a comfortable, loving place where we could start our new life together. It sat at the end of a quiet cul-de-sac, featuring a large yard and a shimmering pool that made us feel blessed that we were still alive and healthy enough to enjoy it. When I first saw the house, I knew it could be home for all three of us.

The split design felt like a gift from heaven. Mia had her own private living space on one side of the home, which gave her the independence she craved as a teenager. At sixteen, she needed space to breathe and process all the changes around her. I wanted her to know that her place in my heart hadn't changed, even though her family, as she knew it, had taken a different path. The separate space meant she could have friends over without feeling that we were watching her every move, and she could retreat when the newness of these new surroundings felt overwhelming. The transition wasn't just about sharing me with a new husband. Mia was also starting at a new high school, facing the challenge of making new friends in a place where everyone already had their groups.

With its thoughtful layout and peaceful setting, the house gave us room to grow into this new version of family. We were different from what we'd been before, but we were becoming something good that honored where we'd all come from while building toward where we wanted to go.

We started an annual garden party for friends, family, neighbors, and co-workers that grew bigger each year. The backyard was perfect for outdoor gatherings, accommodating nearly one hundred people at once. There was live entertainment from the Ken Clemmer and the Back Porch Bandits, dancing, and plenty of food for everyone. The sweetest part of our celebration became our little tradition: each guest brought a small vegetable plant as their "ticket" to the party. We lovingly donated these green gifts to a local assisted living facility, where they found new homes in the residents' community garden. Those dear folks could care for the plants and enjoy the fruits (and vegetables) of their labor.

After Mia graduated from gt high school and moved closer to college, Clayton helped me turn her room into a photo studio. I invested in a professional camera, various lenses, backdrops, lighting equipment, and an Apple computer. Additionally, I enrolled in several classes to learn how to enhance photos using an app called Aperture.

My photography business flourished after attending a popular women's networking luncheon where attendees exchanged business cards to promote their respective businesses. As I sorted through the shoebox full of cards afterward,

I realized that including a photo of each business owner on the cards would enhance marketing efforts. I suggested hosting a photo shoot party at my home, where I could take professional headshots at an affordable price. The rest is history!

In addition to hosting monthly photo parties at my home studio, I also provided on-site photography services at various women's events around town, including eWomen Networking, Pearls of Wisdom, Wow, The Lunch Club, Zocate, The Networking League, Powerful Networking, 9:05 with Christina Wagner and Angel Marie, Foothills Women's Club, and the Ahwatukee chapter of Chat Chew & Chocolate. Clayton became my reluctant "traffic hack" when I attended the monthly Wild Boomer Women Happy Hour. There he was, my husband, sitting at the bar surrounded by enthusiastic women discussing everything from menopause to margaritas. By coming with me, he helped me legally avoid traffic in the HOV lane. Sue Barenholtz, the founder, always slipped him extra drink tickets with a wink, saying, "Hazard pay for being the only rooster in the henhouse." Clayton's smile said it all.

My reputation for enhancing headshots through photo editing was spreading rapidly. I aimed to make the experience comfortable and enjoyable for my clients, using humor to help them relax and smile naturally during their shoots. These home parties became so popular that I had to limit the number of women attending each session. I had a talented professional makeup artist, Ruth Garry, and an excellent jewelry consultant, Kathy Hanchette, who provided valuable insights and curated stunning pieces to complement each outfit. Both women were on-site during the event, ensuring everyone maintained a sophisticated appearance. My charcuterie boards and carefully selected wines became a hit long before they were trendy.

If you want to create a profile photo for social media or an online dating site, here are some tips for choosing flattering clothes that look good in photos.

- Choose solid, vibrant colors; steer clear of plain white

- Choose fitted, tailored clothing

- Avoid wearing low-cut tops or blouses.

- Sleeveless tops aren't always the best option; three-quarter or long-sleeve styles often look better.

- Avoid tops that match your hair color.

- Always choose proper, well-fitting undergarments.

Our 17-year marriage was full of love, laughter, and exciting adventures. During hot summer months in Phoenix, we would escape to our cabin in the Pines. Close friends Kylie and Mike, Lu and Steve, Pipi and Larry, and my sister Marie and her husband Ron would join us for Murder Mystery weekends, scavenger hunts, and breathtaking hikes along the East Verde River.

Early in our marriage, I began another exciting yearly tradition. Every Columbus Day weekend, I planned fun mystery trips to unusual places, which we affectionately called Clayton's Annual Kidnapping Adventure.

One year, I took him to a pickle festival in a tiny town that took its brined cucumbers very seriously. I'm still unsure if Clayton loved it or if the giant pickle costume made him question his life choices... and his marriage vows. As he waddled around in that unwieldy green suit with only his face peeking out, surrounded by pickle enthusiasts debating the merits of dill versus sweet, I caught him giving me a look, but then he cracked a smile and said, "I just want to be the apple of your eye, or should I say your favorite pickle!" But bless that man, he posed for photos with children, judged the pickle-eating contest, and even participated in the pickle relay race. If that's not true love, I don't know what is.

Another year, I took him to Kokopelli Cave, nestled in the cliffs of Farmington, New Mexico. We needed a four-wheel-drive to reach the mountain's peak and then hike what they optimistically called a "trail," but it was more like a dare along the cliff's edge to get to the entrance. I half expected to see an actual goat casually munching on grass, rolling its eyes at our questionable hiking skills. When we reached the cave entrance, we were part mountain climber and part prayer warrior.

Once inside this cave house, we were captivated by its natural beauty and modern amenities. The openings in the rugged rock walls offered stunning views and vibrant sunsets, while a waterfall-style shower and a flagstone hot tub immersed us in the unique experience of a cave dweller's retreat.

We had another amazing trip to the treehouse at The Post Ranch Inn in the heart of Big Sur, California. The calming sound of waves crashing against the cliffs below enriched the experience. During one of our day trips from the treehouse, we attended an outdoor concert at the renowned Esalen Institute, where we were lucky to see Joan Baez perform—one of my favorite singers.

During an unforgettable kidnapping trip, I surprised Clayton with an 80-foot sailboat adventure along the Newport coastline. The boat was equipped with all the comforts one could want and had a skilled captain who was also a talented chef, preparing delicious meals throughout our journey. On that sailboat, we saw amazing sea creatures and enjoyed delicious seafood, creating memories that will last a lifetime.

We also visited several more destinations, including Rancho de la Osa, Arizona's most historic dude ranch; Rancho de los Caballeros, an authentic dude ranch in Wickenburg, Arizona; Tanque Verde Ranch, one of America's traditional cattle and guest ranches in Tucson, Arizona; and the historic Saguaro Lake Guest Ranch, also located in Arizona.

These annual trips were my way of showing gratitude for his kindness and support throughout the year. He was an incredibly generous man, always eager to lend a hand whenever someone needed help. His dedication to helping others inspired me. Clayton was an electrical engineer by profession, but he was also a self-taught master machinist. He knew how to operate every machine tool ever made. He owned not just one but two milling machines, a commercial-grade lathe, drilling and grinding machines, power saws, and a Dillon reloading machine.

I remember when my iron finally broke down. It was old, heavy, and probably qualified for its own social security benefits. After pressing Clayton's five work shirts each week, my arm felt like a wet noodle left in the sun. I tossed that ancient beast into the trash with the ceremonial fanfare it deserved and treated myself to a lightweight model. It was sleek, modern, and practically danced across the fabric. It was the Ferrari of the ironing world.

A few days later, there it was, perched on the kitchen table like a proud trophy: the shiny, glistening old iron, looking better than it had in decades. Clayton had taken it upon himself to resurrect it from the appliance graveyard. He stood there beaming with pride, like Dr. Frankenstein after a particularly successful experiment. "Look, honey, it's back from the dead!" he exclaimed. The man who could fix anything had struck again. I didn't have the heart to tell him I secretly hoped that iron would stay dead and buried. Instead, I smiled, thanked him, and mentioned that I would take it to Beaver Valley in case I needed to press any wrinkles out of our cabin clothes, which was about as likely as me taking up competitive ironing as a hobby.

My persistent cough started in late 2013. Following Clayton's advice, I visited a pulmonologist who diagnosed me with COPD, or Chronic Obstructive Pulmonary Disease. I couldn't help but think about the large amount of secondhand smoke I was exposed to during my first marriage. Tony was a chain smoker and would light each new cigarette from the one he just finished.

Currently, there is no cure for COPD because damaged lung tissue cannot be repaired. After learning that stem cell therapy might improve lung function and reduce COPD-related inflammation, I decided to undergo the treatment. Although I didn't notice any immediate effects, it ultimately proved to be beneficial for me. We decided to take one last trip while I still felt well, uncertain about what my health might be like in the future.

On June 1, 2014, we started a four-month road trip. One of Clayton's bucket list goals was to find his ancestors' burial sites in Stonington, Connecticut, so I planned our route to include that as our stop before heading home. While we were away, my close friend Amy moved into our house to take care of our little dog, Moko. Knowing that our Shih Tzu was in such caring hands was comforting.

I packed my SUV with clothes for various weather conditions and a selection of audiobooks to keep us entertained. Our trip included two weeks in Dallas to spend quality time with Clayton's immediate family, a week at his brother-in-law, Bill's, house in Louisiana, and another week with his cousin Joe and Sue in North Carolina.

We had breathtaking views from the stilt riverfront house we rented for a month along the banks of the Neuse River in North Carolina. One image that remains vivid in my mind is my husband fishing at the end of our private pier. Throughout the month, we enjoyed the bounty of Clayton's fresh catches that enhanced our dinners, including Atlantic croaker and delicate speckled trout. A highlight was when he successfully trapped blue crabs, a delightful treat for me.

Another cherished memory is watching the fleet of sailboats and Sunfish with their brightly colored sails from the kids' summer camp at Don Lee, while sitting on our deck and sipping coffee enriched with Bailey's.

One of the unforgettable weekend trips we took was crossing the Neuse River by ferry to the enchanting Outer Banks Islands. I'll always remember visiting the Wright Brothers Memorial, where we stood in awe of the towering monument that honors the pioneers of flight. We also enjoyed exploring the lighthouses, traveling from one end of the three islands to the other.

We continued our road trip from sunny Florida to Connecticut along the eastern coast, frequently stopping to explore each region's rich and captivating history. We were both excited to find out that Glenn Frey, the legendary former singer and guitarist of the Eagles, was scheduled to perform in Atlantic City. Without hesitation, we changed our itinerary to see one of our favorite artists live. Some of our best moments came from spontaneous decisions.

The final stop on our outbound journey was a month-long stay at a rented harbor house in Stonington, Connecticut. Located by the water, the house provided stunning views of the harbor.

Clayton was determined to find his ancestors' burial grounds. We discovered that the local library had an old area map from the late 1800s. While the current roads were missing, some landmarks still stood out. Clayton took on the task of matching the GPS coordinates, carefully working to connect the past and present. His goal was to guide us to the approximate location of his family's original resting place when they first settled in America.

We ventured into a densely wooded area, pushing through thick brush to carve out a walkable path. Even though it was early morning, the woods stayed dark as the trees blocked the sunlight. After hours of walking, a ray of sunlight broke through a gap in the trees, illuminating a clearing with no leaves. Following the beams of light and crossing the three-foot stone wall, we realized we had stumbled upon the cemetery. Weeds covered the weathered headstones, making it hard to read the names, but we both knew that we had found the long-lost graves.

We discovered a peaceful fishing village near Mystic called Noank during our many day trips around Stonington. While exploring the area, we stumbled upon a Historical Society Store Museum and learned that this was the site where Amelia Earhart got married in 1931. On another side trip, we toured the nuclear-powered Nautilus submarine in New London and enjoyed a riverboat cruise on the Becky Thatcher along the Connecticut River. We also visited the Steam Train in Essex and found Gillette Castle fascinating. Additionally, we spent some time walking on the beaches in Rhode Island. Our favorite happy hour was at Saltwater Farms Vineyard, and we savored dining at various charming spots in Mystic.

On our way home, we enjoyed a wonderful chance to meet my sister and brother-in-law at their week-long timeshare near Niagara Falls. It was our first time seeing the falls, and Clayton and I were amazed by their breathtaking beauty. As night arrived, we went to the Canadian side, where the waterfalls were beautifully lit up with a dazzling display of colors.

Heading south, we made a quick stop in Cleveland to visit Amy's mom. We wanted to thank Marietta for her daughter's loving care of our little Moko, which allowed us to enjoy this vacation.

I was excited to reconnect with my first cousins, Jeanna and Jack, in Southern Illinois. It had been many years since I last saw them, and I was filled with nostalgia. I was eager to share laughter and stories that shaped our childhood.

Our joyful reunion was unexpectedly cut short when Clayton, looking a little pale and tired, insisted we go home early. His worry about his health worried me, so we hopped into the car without delay. The drive home was a blur; we hurried to get back as quickly as we could.

When we finally reached home, Clayton collapsed onto the couch, his face twisted with pain. I watched him clutch his lower back, and fear swept over me like a cold wave. Something was terribly wrong. I helped him into the car, my hands trembling and my heart pounding against my ribs as I drove to the hospital. With every turn, my worry deepened.

The hospital felt cold and lifeless compared to the warmth of our home. After endless waiting, the CT scan results came back. When the doctor said, "stage 4 metastatic cancer," the words struck me like a punch to the chest. I couldn't breathe. Those terrible words hung in the air between us, crushing the peaceful life we had built together. In that moment, everything I thought I knew about the future simply disappeared.

For two months, Clayton stayed in the hospital undergoing chemotherapy and radiation. Then the doctors told us he could come home to spend his final days there. During that last month at home, I became everything: nurse, caregiver, and heartbroken wife all at once. I learned to feed him when he couldn't hold a spoon, to mix his medications to manage his increasing pain, and to change his colostomy bag every day. But nothing prepared me for watching the vibrant man I loved slowly slip away, gradually fading into a shadow of his former self. Each day felt like losing him all over again.

Three months after his diagnosis, I held his frail hand for the last time. The man I loved was gone, and it felt like my heart had shattered into a million pieces. Throughout my life, I've faced many challenges, job losses, disappointments, and moments of self-doubt, but nothing could have prepared me for the deep emotional pain and suffering. Losing Clayton taught me that grief is its own kind of breaking, one that changes you forever.

Yet, amidst the sorrow, my furry friend, Moko, became a beacon of comfort and solace during my darkest moments. Our sweet, fluffy Shih Tzu was more than just a pet; she was pure love wrapped in soft fur. With her big, soulful eyes and playful spirit, Moko seemed to sense my pain. She stayed right beside me, offering the kind of quiet comfort that only animals can give.

The first night after Clayton passed, Moko sat on the floor looking up at me with those big pleading eyes, asking to be lifted up. She had always slept in her little bed on the floor next to Clayton's side. But that night, I realized she was grieving too. So, I picked her up, nestled her beside me, and whispered, "I know you miss him too, baby girl. You can sleep here with me, but just for tonight." That "one night' became every night. I like to think Clayton is somewhere watching us, probably chuckling at how quickly his faithful dog claimed his spot in our bed. Moko needed me. And I needed her. Caring for her felt like holding onto a piece of him, like love finding a way to continue even after everything had changed.

Moko could sense my feelings. She knew when I needed her comforting cuddles. Whenever she wanted to play, she would drop her favorite toy at my feet and patiently look up at me with her expressive eyes until I agreed. I must admit, she trained me well.

My three wedding rings tell the story of my journey through love and loss. The first, a simple gold band that never quite fit, connected me to a world of excitement and danger. The second, a beautiful diamond-studded band that kept spinning around my finger, linked me to years of family joy but ultimately couldn't stay steady. The third was a perfect fit that remained securely in place until death parted us, bringing me the truest love I would ever know. Each ring marked a chapter in my life, each taught me something essential, and together they shaped the woman I am today, someone who knows that love, in all its forms, is worth every moment of joy and every tear of grief.

Chapter 2 - Eliminating Skeletons

I keep my closet neat and organized, which gives me a sense of control in a world that often feels out of control. I sort my clothes into groups: shirts, pants, dresses, and activewear, and I arrange them by color within each group. This method makes putting together outfits easy. To maximize space, I fold and store my T-shirts, place purses on the top shelf for easy access, and arrange shoes in clear storage bins.

Organizing my first husband's clothes took some time, but I eventually became skilled at it. What truly surprised me was the amount of space Tony claimed in our closet. I appreciate a man who takes pride in his appearance, but seriously, did he think we were opening a Western wear store? I had to squeeze my outfits into one corner while he claimed the entire walk-in closet as his personal western runway.

It's said, "Behind every successful man is a great woman." In my case, I was his personal stylist, therapist, and color consultant. Tony was as fashion-savvy as a potato in a tuxedo. So, I took it upon myself to curate his daily wardrobe. I meticulously coordinated shirts, pants, and the perfect shoes; he'd march in, pull my perfectly coordinated hanger out like he'd struck gold, and say, "Thanks, babe, you're a lifesaver."

After Tony passed away, I inherited the entire closet. I must admit, it was exciting to have all that space. So, I did what any reasonable widow would do: I went shopping! Now, that might sound heartless, but I prefer to call it "retail therapy with a grief discount." Sometimes healing comes with a shopping bag and a receipt.

The homeless shelter was absolutely thrilled with my donation of Tony's western collection. Phoenix's homeless population suddenly looked like they were extras in a Clint Eastwood film called "The Good, The Bad, and The Hungry." These street beggars could have been mistaken for the "Ruggedly Handsome Posse," but without the six-shooters. I like to think Tony would have appreciated that his clothes found such a worthy second act.

My second marriage ended in divorce, and Danny couldn't pack his things fast enough. I was left with the remnants he no longer wanted. Instead of letting these items weigh me down like emotional anchors, I realized there was only one sensible option: to donate everything he left behind. Being the mischievous soul that I am, I couldn't resist tucking little notes into the pockets of the clothes before parting with them. I wrote gems like: "The previous owner of this shirt was more traveled than a hotel suitcase," and "Warning: These jeans belonged to a man who thought keeping his junk inside them was optional," and my personal favorite: "These pants have seen more action than a popcorn machine at movie night!" Adding that touch of humor to the whole cleaning-out process wasn't just a powerful therapeutic release; it was downright exhilarating. Somewhere out there, strangers were finding my little truth bombs, and that thought warmed me up better than hot chocolate on a winter day.

When my third husband, Clayton, passed away, grief came in waves: deep sadness, simmering anger, paralyzing fear, and ultimately, acceptance. This emotional rollercoaster didn't happen overnight; it was a process, like learning to dance with tears and occasionally screaming into my pillow. It took months before I felt comfortable making major decisions.

I cleared Clayton's clothes from our closet during the first month. I packed and labeled his belongings with the care of someone preserving precious artifacts and stored everything in the garage like a shrine I wasn't quite ready to visit. Some skeletons take longer to eliminate than others, and that's perfectly okay because it's not in your closet.

I took nearly two years to decide to downsize and sell our home.

Before hosting the estate sale, I invited family members to choose items they wanted to keep. Clayton's two sons came at my request to help sell items from his man cave, that sacred temple of tools and machinery where he performed his mechanical miracles. During the sale, a man who stopped by commented, "It's incredible that one person could have the knowledge and skill to operate such a vast array of machinery and tools." If only he knew how many of Clayton's friends had brought him broken tools to repair, turning our garage into the neighborhood fix-it clinic. He never charged for these repairs, although he didn't mind accepting a nice bottle of bourbon in exchange for his efforts.

Clayton was an electrical engineer by profession and had more skills than a televised home improvement show. In addition to operating various commercial machinery and tools, he enjoyed making wine and beer. I'll never forget when he embraced his inner winemaker and crafted a five-gallon glass jug of ruby-red prickly pear wine. However, as he made his grand entrance from the basement to the kitchen table upstairs, he lost his grip, and the glass container slipped from his hands. It didn't just fall; it exploded like a grenade of sticky magenta liquid, sending glass shrapnel so far that pieces even slid under the refrigerator across the room.

When I hurried into the kitchen to see what had caused the crash, it looked like a wine bomb had exploded! Clayton was covered in bright magenta wine from head to toe. Honestly, it resembled a scene straight out of the *I Love Lucy* show. We laughed until we cried, all the while knowing we had a big mess to clean up.

Clayton's absence for nearly two years prompted me to make a major decision. I decided to sell my home and move to our summer cabin in the Pines. Since the cabin was fully furnished, I didn't need to bring much. However, I did not anticipate the challenges posed by the winter weather.

Shortly after I moved into the cabin, a snowstorm that felt like it came straight out of a disaster movie struck the area. The most sensible option was to return to Phoenix, but my car was buried under a thick blanket of snow. Even the entrance gate was frozen shut. Cut off from cell service, I felt helpless and frustrated about my decision to make this place my permanent home.

The cabin is a perfect summer retreat, the key word being SUMMER. It is situated beneath the Mogollon Rim (pronounced Moggy-on), surrounded by the majestic mountains of Coconino National Forest. This diverse region features Ponderosa Pine forests and even some alpine tundra. During the summer, you can relax on the deck and enjoy the tranquil sounds of birds singing and a nearby river flowing. I had moved from Chicago to Phoenix specifically to escape the frigid winters. Now trapped in the cold and snow, my anger surged, giving me the strength to motivate myself.

First, I tackled the snow-covered car with a broom. Then, I grabbed a shovel and scraped the packed ice and snow around the gate, cursing with creativity that would make a sailor blush. Using all my strength, I pushed the manual gate open just enough to drive my car through. After skidding and sliding along the treacherous icy back roads, I finally hit the freshly plowed highway. I was home free; except I didn't have a home to go to. After drying my tears and regaining my composure, I made another significant decision. Soon after, I bought a small patio home near my kids. That choice gave me the best of both worlds: winters in Phoenix and summers in the Pines.

How to Get Started Eliminating Skeletons

Cleaning out a loved one's closet, drawers, and cabinets can be an emotional experience. Their familiar scent may linger on clothing, triggering memories and strong feelings to resurface. Fortunately, there's no set timeline for packing up and giving away their belongings. Some people dive right in, while others hold onto their loved one's possessions for years. This is a personal decision, so choose what feels right for you.

When you are ready, here are some tips:

- Plan ahead. Start with smaller projects to avoid feeling overwhelmed. The bathroom may be easier to manage than a closet.

- Access your support system. You may have a close friend, neighbor, or family member who is willing to help. You don't have to go through this alone. Invite a trusted, compassionate friend over when sorting through more sentimental items. It'll be nice to have someone there to share memories, listen to stories, and help you process strong emotions—or just to keep handing you tissues.

- Implement a keep, toss, sell, donate system using labeled bins, bags, or boxes. Deciding on items with sentimental value might be difficult. Place them in a "24-hour box." Sleep on it and make your decision in the morning. Just remember, you can't keep everything.

- Please take pictures of items you're ready to part with, but want to remember how they look.

- Be time sensitive. Don't give up on yourself once you decide to eliminate and purge. Set a completion date, knowing there may be a few emotional setbacks. A deadline will help you stay on track.

- Deal with the paperwork. Naturally, you'll want to keep important documents. Create a filing system for medical records, bank statements, tax returns, birth certificates, passports, and diplomas.

- Most clothes can be donated to a local charity. You can also take higher-end clothing in excellent condition to a local consignment shop. Some consignment shops require a pre-scheduled appointment to review your items. Make sure your items are clean, pressed, and on hangers.

- You might want to consider passing your jewelry down to your children, grandchildren, nieces, nephews, and the deceased's friends. This can be done immediately or specifically noted in a will for later distribution.

- China and glassware can also be passed down, donated, or consigned.

- Value the journals and correspondence. Save any journals, diaries, or letters in case you or a family member chooses to document your loved one's story someday, as these could serve as historical records.

- Maintain harmony. Before disposing of items that belonged to your deceased spouse, please consult not only your children but also any children from before your marriage. Don't assume that biological or stepchildren won't be interested in these belongings. Certain items may hold sentimental value, and they would appreciate the opportunity to receive them or even to be asked about them.

Death Cleaning is another option when you are removing skeletons from a loved one you've lost. It is a thoughtful way to organize your belongings while you're still alive. The goal is simple: reduce the burden on your family and friends after you're gone. Sometimes we hold onto things that hurt us. Maybe it's a gift that reminds us of someone we've lost. These items can keep old wounds open. Death cleaning gives you a chance to heal. Take your time. Every item you own has a story. That old sweater, the family photo, the painting on your wall. As you decide what to keep, you can share these stories with the people you love. Go through each item slowly. Ask yourself: "Does this serve me anymore?" If the answer is no, you can choose to let it go along with the pain it carries. This process can be deeply freeing. You're not just clearing your space; you're clearing emotional weight you may have carried for years.

Eliminating skeletons isn't just about cleaning out the closet; it's about making room in your heart to keep moving forward, one sock drawer at a time.

Chapter 3 - Colonoscopy Cruise

Looking back on my past, I realize that any of my former husbands would have stood by my side, offering support during necessary medical procedures. Their presence gave me comfort that I now miss deeply. However, living alone means you rely on a family member, friend, neighbor, or Uber driver to get you to those important outpatient appointments. I still find it difficult to handle health procedures on my own, even when they involve parts of my body I'd prefer not to discuss with casual acquaintances.

It wasn't surprising when the doctor told me it was time for another colonoscopy, one of life's unavoidable and unwelcome rites of passage after turning 50. In those cheerful medical pamphlets, they don't tell you that the procedure is easy; the preparation deserves its place in Dante's Inferno.

The night before the big day felt like a mini endurance test as I drank endless MoviPrep. The instructions were written by someone with a great sense of humor, stating that "a loose, watery bowel movement MAY result after you drink it." This concoction was more than a potent liquid laxative; it acted like Drano for the digestive system, flushing everything out until nothing remained. Then, you start eliminating food that you haven't even eaten yet! I do not want to be too graphic, but let me ask, "Have you ever seen a space shuttle launch?" This is the MoviPrep experience, with YOU as the shuttle.

As I sat on the porcelain throne, the only comfort I had during my body's purge was resting my head on a plush pillow on a bar stool directly in front of me. I had turned my bathroom into a makeshift command center, complete with magazines, my phone, and enough toilet paper to last through another pandemic.

But this wasn't my first experience with this particular medical procedure. My doctor's initial reluctance to perform the colonoscopy made this time different. Since my diagnosis of chronic obstructive pulmonary disease (COPD), I have struggled to maintain my weight. When your lungs don't function properly, your body has to work harder to breathe, which can burn up to ten times more calories than usual. It's perhaps the world's least enjoyable weight loss program. COPD, characterized by shortness of breath and a persistent cough, can lead to a reduced appetite and eventual weight loss. In severe cases, it may even cause cachexia, a serious metabolic wasting condition commonly seen in patients with advanced cancer.

Because I was so underweight, my doctor recommended we wait until I gained a few pounds.

Mission accomplished. How? I'll get to that.

A way to gain weight is by taking a cruise. Cruise ships are floating all-you-can-eat buffets where calories don't matter, and elastic waistbands become your best friends. I was lucky to be part of The Wild Boomer Women, which offered an all-inclusive wine cruise to Santa Barbara—perfect timing! Sue Barenholtz founded Wild Boomer Women in 2008 as a social group for baby boomer women looking for fun and camaraderie. This wonderful group organized monthly happy hours, various activities, and travel events. It felt like Lady Luck had designed it just for me: three delicious meals a day, plenty of snacks, and enough wine to satisfy any connoisseur.

As if I needed more temptation, the nine other fabulous boomers on the trip were determined to help me pack on the calories. These women took my weight gain mission as a personal challenge, constantly showing up with plates of desserts throughout the journey. "Bobbie, you simply must try the chocolate lava cake," Janette insisted one evening, sliding a decadent dessert in front of me. "Doctor's orders!" The others nodded in agreement, clinking their wine glasses to toast my health. With friends like these, failure wasn't an option.

I returned home five pounds heavier and ready for surgery, calling the trip the Colonoscopy Cruise. Now, I was lying on that cold gurney in pre-op, my culinary adventure earning me a ticket to this medical procedure. As I waited for the doctor, I couldn't help but smile, thinking about how those Wild Boomer Women would laugh if they could see me now. The destination of our celebratory cruise is this sterile hospital room.

My thoughts were interrupted as the conversations of the patients on either side of my curtained enclosure became clearer. To my left, a man expressed his frustration, insisting he would leave if someone didn't take him into surgery within the next five minutes. His wife tried to comfort him, but he was very upset about the long wait. I thought about reminding him about the Nuclear Laxative he would have to drink again if he canceled, but decided that might not be appropriate coming from a stranger behind a curtain. So, I simply lay there and listened to the other voices around me.

I overheard a woman to my right talking on her cell phone. Her tone was weak and unsteady as she gave final instructions to a loved one in case she passed away during the medical procedure. Of course, it was a possibility, as complications could arise from anesthesia, her heart could fail, or they might discover tumors or cancer during the procedure. I knew I shouldn't let such thoughts consume me; it was a moment to focus on my own situation. Instead, I found myself reflecting on the laughter and camaraderie from the Colonoscopy Cruise that led me to this point, surrounded by women who understood that sometimes friendship means force-feeding someone chocolate cake for medicinal purposes.

Finally, a young male nurse pulled the curtains aside and wheeled me into the operating room. Given what that job entailed, he had the enthusiasm of someone who clearly enjoyed his work a little too much. The smiling doctor asked what music I wanted to hear. I briefly considered requesting "Come Sail Away" by Styx in honor of my recent cruise, but settled on "Moon River" or "Beethoven's Last Movement."

The next thing I remember is waking up after a successful procedure and hearing that my colon had passed with flying colors. I considered asking what the colors were, but ultimately decided against it.

It was time to celebrate with a rich, creamy strawberry shake! As I sipped my reward, I made a mental note to text the Wild Boomer Women group chat. After all, they deserved to know that their dessert efforts had paid off—their mission to fatten me up had not only succeeded but had possibly saved my life. Sometimes the best medicine isn't what the doctor prescribes, but the friends who encourage you to enjoy that piece of chocolate cake.

Chapter 4 - One Plate, One Fork

Good food, rather than junk food, shapes our physical and emotional well-being. I am currently co-writing a recipe book with Carolyn Golden, *One Plate, One Fork*, which features "Mood Meals" designed to soothe emotional hunger from the heart rather than the stomach. Details on the release date will be posted on my website, bobbiebennett.com.

Solitary dining can feel lonely and depressing, especially for many recent widows, widowers, and divorcees, as it serves as a painful reminder of their partner's absence. However, dining alone can also offer a sense of freedom. You don't have to cater to anyone else's preferences when deciding whether to go out to eat, cook at home, or buy ready-made food. You can be more assertive about the foods you choose.

I have never relied on anyone to cook or take care of me. I've always been independent and self-sufficient. Embracing the art of cooking and eating alone is truly freeing for me! I have the freedom to enjoy any food, at any time, and anywhere. For example, I might have a veggie omelet for dinner and steak and potatoes for breakfast. I don't have to please anyone but myself, which is empowering.

For those recently widowed or divorced, finding the motivation to eat can be tough at first, and preparing meals for one might feel intimidating and unfamiliar. It's often easier to just have a cup of coffee and a muffin for breakfast, grab a hot dog from Costco for lunch, and microwave a frozen entrée for dinner. While these choices are fine occasionally, regularly skipping meals and neglecting proper nutrition can harm your health and figure.

One of the most health-promoting, cost-effective, and confidence-boosting things you can do is cook your own meals. Maybe the partner you lost was the main cook, and you lack basic cooking skills. That's a reasonable challenge, but it's only a temporary setback. You can create a healthy, delicious dish or meal by reading a recipe, following directions, or watching a cooking video.

As I previously mentioned, I learned to cook authentic Italian dishes from my former Italian mother-in-law. She generously shared her family's secret recipe for "Sunday Gravy" with me, a spaghetti sauce I use in many different ways. She was right when she said that the gravy is the key to making any Italian meal delicious. I always keep several gallon-sized freezer bags filled with her secret sauce neatly stacked in my freezer. The next chapter, "Mama Says Mangia," features some of her best recipes. I believe they are easy to learn and will bring you and others comfort, nourishment, and joy.

Since my husband, Clayton, passed away, I've maintained my shopping routines. I still venture through the crowds at Costco to buy bulk meat, fish, or poultry. But once home, I divide, date, and label single portions before freezing. This helps me plan my daily meals and prepare vegetable sides using ingredients I enjoy, rather than staring blankly into the refrigerator as if it's an archaeological dig.

When dining alone at home, it's important to enjoy the experience. Avoid using plain paper plates; instead, take pride in setting your table for meals. This simple gesture can turn an ordinary meal into a small celebration of self-care. Whether you choose to eat at the dining table or have casual meals on the couch while watching your favorite show, that's perfectly fine.

I soon realized that being single didn't mean I had to eat alone forever. I often make a little extra and invite a friend or neighbor to join me. Good food combined with friendly conversation makes for an enjoyable dining experience.

Holiday gatherings and special occasions have become treasured traditions, especially now that my grandkids want to help with the preparations. Through these shared moments, each meal becomes more than just food; it turns into a celebration of love, tradition, and family bonds.

Several years ago, I discovered that I am allergic to monosodium glutamate (MSG). I had to change my eating habits to avoid debilitating migraines, no more processed, packaged, or fast foods.

I prepare most of my meals from scratch, using fresh ingredients for meal planning and making my own chicken broth. I freeze the homemade broth in one-cup portions with freezer bags for easier storage. Besides my gravy, I also batch-cook soups and store them in smaller portions in the freezer.

I keep pre-sliced bread in the freezer and take out what I need to prevent the loaf from going stale or getting moldy.

My pantry is stocked with canned tomatoes, beans, and tuna, as well as dried herbs and spices, nuts, cold-pressed olive oil, balsamic vinegar, pasta, rice, and flour. Having these essential staples on hand allows me to quickly prepare a healthy meal.

Freezing

When you eat alone, learning how to effectively freeze meals can be very helpful. You can roast a chicken, grill burgers, or cook a pot of stew, then divide the food into smaller portions to freeze for later. Using freezer bags saves space in your freezer. Be sure to label and date each bag and stack them flat. Alternatively, you can use food storage containers. I find that the Snapware brand from Pyrex holds up well in the freezer, is dishwasher-safe, and can be used in the microwave.

Here's a helpful tip for freezing food. After cooking and slicing, let the food cool on the counter. Then, divide it into smaller portions and put them into containers or freezer bags. Use a bold marker to label and date them. Next, place the containers in the refrigerator. Wait! The next day, move the labeled containers into the freezer. Voila! You won't have to worry about bacteria growing in your food if you let everything cool *completely* before freezing. See? You're already becoming a pro!

Dining Out

A few years ago, a new restaurant chain in Phoenix offered slow-roasted chicken paired with a variety of delicious side dishes. I was excited to try it, especially after the manager assured me they hadn't added any MSG to the meals. I ended up ordering several items to take home. Unfortunately, I suffered a severe migraine and was bedridden for three days after eating the food. To my surprise, everything I ordered contained MSG, although the manager was technically correct in stating that none had been "added" at the restaurant. The MSG seasoning in the product was infused at the factory, as confirmed by their corporate headquarters. When I submitted a complaint to the company, they sent me ten complimentary coupons redeemable at any of their locations. I passed those along to anyone interested in them.

Some restaurants offer a "buy one dinner, get one at half price" deal. I decided to take advantage of the savings by ordering both meals and requesting the second meal be packed for takeout so I could enjoy it later. However, not all restaurants allow this. They rely on having two customers dining in person, hoping that they'll order appetizers, desserts, and drinks to increase the total bill. I recommend checking in advance to avoid any confusion.

I enjoy cooking my own meals, but when I dine out, I prefer gourmet restaurants. They make their dishes from scratch and avoid adding MSG, so I can order anything from their menu without worrying about harmful ingredients. Although it may cost more, the peace of mind is worth it. Dining at an upscale restaurant also gives me a sense of comfort and relaxation.

Here are some tips to improve your dining experience, making it more comfortable and enjoyable:

Solo Dining

If you're dining alone, ask for a table for two. This helps prevent being seated in less desirable spots like near the kitchen door or bus station. Request a table with a view when possible. Keep in mind that solo diners deserve the same quality experience as larger groups.

Group Dining

- When dining with friends, ask for separate checks at the start of your meal. This avoids awkward bill-splitting talks and makes payment easier for everyone.

- For bigger groups, consider making reservations ahead of time, especially at busy restaurants.

- Be mindful of group volume to maintain a pleasant atmosphere for other diners.

-

Building Relationships

- Return to restaurants you enjoy and build rapport with staff. Being recognized leads to a more personalized experience.

- Engage in friendly conversation with staff when appropriate, but respect their time and responsibilities.

- Remember the names of regular servers or hosts; this small gesture shows appreciation.

Etiquette and Tipping

- Unless the service is truly poor, leave a generous tip if you can. Staff remember generous customers and often provide better service on future visits.

- Be patient during busy times and clearly and politely communicate any special requests.

- Give specific, positive feedback to staff and management when you have an exceptional experience.

Maximizing Your Experience

- Try visiting during off-peak hours for a more relaxed atmosphere and attentive service.

- Feel free to ask for recommendations, servers usually have great insights on menu highlights.

- Think about signing up for restaurant loyalty programs at your favorite spots to enjoy exclusive deals and events.

These improved tips should make your dining experiences more enjoyable and comfortable!

Chapter 5 - Mama Says Mangia!

I have expressed my desire to continue my legacy. One way my family can preserve my memory and heritage is by using my recipes and feeling my spirit in each dish. Here are some of my favorites, thanks to my Italian mother-in-law.

Spaghetti Salad

The great thing about this cold salad is that it tastes even better the next day, so you can enjoy this meal twice!

For the salad:

1 pound of spaghetti

1 cup cherry tomatoes, cut in half

1 diced cucumber

1 red bell pepper, diced into small pieces

Half a red onion, finely chopped

1 cup shredded carrots

½ cup black olives, sliced

½ cup shredded mozzarella cheese (optional)

¼ cup fresh parsley, chopped

For the dressing:

½ cup olive oil

¼ cup red wine vinegar

2 tablespoons lemon juice

2 tablespoons sugar (or honey for a natural sweetener)

1 teaspoon dried oregano

1 teaspoon garlic powder

Salt and pepper, to taste

Directions:

Step 1: Cook the pasta

Bring a large pot of salted water to a boil. Cook the spaghetti according to the package instructions until al dente. Drain and rinse lightly under cold water to stop the cooking. Toss with a little olive oil to prevent sticking.

Step 2: Prep the veggies

As the pasta cooks, chop all the vegetables and set them aside.

Step 3: Make the dressing

In a small bowl, whisk together olive oil, red wine vinegar, lemon juice, sugar, oregano, garlic powder, salt, and pepper. Taste and adjust the seasoning as needed.

Step 4: Assemble the salad

In a large mixing bowl, combine the cooled pasta, cherry tomatoes, cucumber, red bell pepper, red onion, carrots, black olives, and parsley. Drizzle the dressing over the salad and gently toss to mix.

Step 5: Chill and serve

Cover the salad and refrigerate for at least 1 to 2 hours to allow the flavors to meld. Before serving, stir the salad well and garnish with shredded mozzarella cheese if desired.

Grandma's Honeycrisp Apple Salad

Ingredients

4 large Honeycrisp apples (washed and diced)

1 cup seedless red grapes, halved

2 ribs of celery, thinly sliced

1/2 cup walnuts (chopped)

1/2 cup dried cranberries

3/4 cup light mayonnaise

1 1/2 tablespoons white sugar

Directions

In a large bowl, combine the chopped apples, grapes, celery, walnuts, and dried cranberries. In a separate bowl, mix the light mayonnaise and sugar until smooth. Pour the mayonnaise mixture over the fruit and toss until everything is well combined. Refrigerate for 1 hour before serving.

Strawberry Feta Salad

Ingredients:

4 cups baby spinach

1 tablespoon extra-virgin olive oil

2 tablespoons balsamic vinegar

1/8 teaspoon black pepper

2 cups sliced strawberries

1 cup walnuts

1/2 cup Feta cheese

Instructions:

Place the spinach, olive oil, balsamic vinegar, and black pepper into a large salad bowl. Use tongs to toss the ingredients and combine them. Add the sliced strawberries and walnuts to the salad bowl. Toss the salad again to mix in the strawberries and walnuts. Gently add the Feta cheese and toss the salad.

Serve and enjoy!

Strawberry Crunch Salad

Ingredients

Salad

⅔ cup sliced or slivered almonds

3 tablespoons sugar

10 ounces arugula greens

8 ounces strawberries, hulled and quartered or chopped

1 avocado, chopped

2 ounces crumbled goat cheese,

⅓ cup roasted salted pistachios, chopped

Champagne Vinaigrette

3 tablespoons champagne vinegar

Juice of 1/2 lemon

2 tablespoons honey

1 teaspoon Dijon mustard

1 garlic clove, freshly grated

pinch kosher salt and pepper

½ cup olive oil

Instructions

Place the almonds in a nonstick skillet over medium heat. Stir in the sugar and cook, stirring frequently, until the sugar melts and becomes caramelized, coating all the almonds - about 6 to 8 minutes. Don't take your eyes off this, as they can burn quickly! Transfer the almonds to a piece of parchment paper to cool. Break them into pieces if they clump together.

Toss the arugula with a pinch of salt and pepper in a large bowl. Then add the strawberries, avocado, goat cheese, pistachios, and sugared almonds.

Champagne vinaigrette dressing

Combine vinegar, honey, lemon juice, Dijon mustard, garlic, salt, and pepper in a large bowl and whisk until blended. Gradually add the olive oil while continuously whisking until the dressing is well combined. Store in the refrigerator for up to one week.

Drizzle the dressing on the salad and toss well. Serve immediately!

Mom's Spinach Salad

This salad can serve as a main course because it contains hard-boiled eggs, which are a great source of protein. For the best flavor, use only fresh ingredients. Add the dressing just five minutes before serving to keep the salad crisp.

When invited to a dinner party, it is always thoughtful to ask if you can contribute to the meal. I'm frequently asked to bring this spinach salad because it's a crowd-pleaser.

Salad ingredients:

10-ounce bag of baby spinach

Hard-boiled eggs (one per person)

One pound of cooked, drained, and crumbled crispy bacon

Bean sprouts (optional)

Sliced strawberries (optional).

Dressing ingredients:

1 cup olive oil, preferably organic

¼ cup ketchup

¼ cup wine vinegar

¼ cup sugar

Refrigerate the dressing for at least one hour before serving.

Combine the salad with the dressing and serve it.

Grandma's Pickled Cucumbers

Grandma would chill this overnight before serving.

Ingredients:

1 cup sugar

1 cup water

4 cucumbers, peeled, sliced thin

½ cup apple cider vinegar

1 tablespoon oil

1 tablespoon celery seed

Directions:

In a large bowl, soak the prepared cucumbers in ice water with a pinch of salt for 1 to 2 hours to make them crispy. Combine water and sugar in a pot and cook over medium heat until the mixture is clear, stirring constantly. Allow to cool. Add vinegar, oil, and celery seed. Drain cucumbers, pat them dry, and combine with the vinegar mixture. Chill overnight.

Lemon Pasta

One of the great things about having cooked pasta in the refrigerator is that you can whip up a sauce and have a delicious meal ready in minutes.

Some of my out-of-state friends passing through Arizona decided to stop by to say hello. They were so impressed with my lemon pasta dish that I added it to my book. I hope you enjoy it as much as they did.

Ingredients:

1 pound spaghetti noodles

4 tablespoons unsalted butter or ghee (clarified butter)

4 lemons, zested*

Juice from 2 lemons

¼ cup half-and-half or heavy cream

½ cup grated Parmesan cheese, plus more for serving

Salt and black pepper to taste

1 cup pasta water

*Zest is the outermost layer of the lemon peel that contains natural oils and flavor. You can use a cheese grater with small holes if you don't own a lemon zester.

Tip: Pasta water is a crucial ingredient, so it's important to save at least a cup of it before draining the pasta.

Pasta:

Begin by bringing a large pot of salted water to a boil.

Add the spaghetti to the boiling water and cook until al dente or just tender to the bite (1-2 minutes less than the package cooking instructions).

Reserve 1 cup or more of pasta water after the pasta has finished cooking.

Drain the pasta.

Sauce:

While the pasta is cooking, you can prepare the sauce.

In a large skillet over medium heat, melt the butter and add the lemon zest and juice.

Add ½ cup of pasta water and bring it to a low simmer.

Season the sauce with salt and pepper to taste.

Combine:

Add the cooked pasta to the skillet and toss to coat with the sauce.

Stir in the cream and ¼ cup of pasta water, or more if the pasta is too thick.

Turn off the heat and stir in the Parmesan cheese.

Serve the pasta with freshly ground black pepper and extra Parmesan if desired.

Baked Ziti with Sausage

Ingredients:

cooking spray

1 (16 ounces) package ziti pasta

1 pound mild or hot bulk Italian sausage

1 (15-ounce) container ricotta cheese

1 large egg

2 teaspoons minced garlic

1 teaspoon dried oregano

½ teaspoon salt

½ teaspoon ground black pepper

1 (26-ounce) jar spaghetti sauce, divided (pre-made or store-bought)

¾ cup freshly grated Parmesan cheese

1 teaspoon crushed red pepper flakes

1 sprig fresh basil (optional)

Directions

Preheat the oven to 350°F. Lightly spray a 9x13-inch baking dish.

Bring a large pot of slightly salted water to a rolling boil over high heat. Stir in ziti and return to a boil. Cook the pasta uncovered, stirring occasionally, until it is cooked through but still firm to the bite, about 8 minutes. Drain well.

While the pasta cooks, heat a large skillet over medium heat. Add the sausage and cook, stirring occasionally, until browned, about 10 minutes. Drain the sausage and set it aside.

In a large bowl, combine ricotta, egg, garlic, and oregano until smooth. Mix in pasta, sausage, salt, pepper, crushed red pepper flakes, and half a jar of spaghetti sauce until well blended.

Spread 1/3 of the spaghetti sauce from the jar onto the bottom of the prepared baking dish. Add half of the pasta mixture, followed by half of the remaining spaghetti sauce and half of the shredded cheese. Repeat this process one more time with the remaining pasta, sauce, and cheese. Finally, sprinkle parmesan cheese and basil on top, then cover the dish tightly with aluminum foil.

Bake in the preheated oven for about 20 minutes. Uncover and return to the oven, baking for an additional 5 to 10 minutes, until the cheese is melted.

Allow to sit for about 10 minutes before serving.

Chicken Piccata

Ingredients:

    1¼ pounds thinly sliced chicken breasts

    Salt and pepper for seasoning

    2 tablespoons olive oil

    ¼ cup fresh lemon juice

    ¼ cup reduced-sodium chicken broth

    3 tablespoons capers in brine, rinsed

    2 tablespoons butter or ghee (clarified butter)

    2 tablespoons roughly chopped parsley, more for optional garnish

Preparation:

Season the chicken with salt and pepper on both sides.

Heat a large skillet over medium-high heat. Add one tablespoon of olive oil to the pan and let it warm up. Place two pieces of chicken in the skillet and cook for 3 minutes on each side. Once cooked, transfer the chicken to a plate and cover it. Add another tablespoon of olive oil to the pan and cook the remaining chicken breasts the same way. Finally, transfer all the cooked chicken to a plate and cover it again.

Add ¼ cup of fresh lemon juice, ¼ cup of broth, and 2 to 3 tablespoons of capers to the pan, deglazing the bottom by scraping up the small brown bits with a spatula. Bring to a gentle boil and return all the chicken to the pan. Reduce the heat and let it simmer for about 5 minutes, until the sauce has thickened and reduced by half. Turn off the heat, remove the chicken, and transfer it to a serving platter, reserving all the sauce in the pan. Add two tablespoons of butter to the pan, whisk or swirl to melt, and mix the butter into the sauce.

Taste the sauce and adjust with extra salt, pepper, and lemon to suit your preference. Stir in the chopped parsley quickly to mix. Pour the sauce over the plated chicken and garnish with more chopped parsley if desired. This recipe makes four servings.

Cacio e Pepe: Pasta with Cheese and Pepper

This dish is my quick and easy go-to meal. I use some *al dente* pasta I keep in my refrigerator; all I need to do is prepare this super simple sauce. Just add a colorful, fresh salad, and your meal is complete. Bon appétit!

Ingredients:

2 to 3 tablespoons kosher salt

¾ pound uncooked spaghetti or linguine

1 tablespoon freshly ground black pepper high-quality olive oil

1 cup reserved pasta water

1 ½ cups finely grated Pecorino Romano cheese

Tip: For each gallon of water (or 4 quarts, the amount needed for a whole box of pasta), add 2 to 3 tablespoons of kosher salt. Make sure to add the salt to the water before cooking the pasta.

Remember, pasta water is a crucial ingredient; be sure to save a cup of it before draining the pasta.

Pasta:

Fill a large pot with water, add 3 to 4 tablespoons of kosher salt, and bring to a boil over high heat.

Add the pasta and cook according to the package instructions.

Drain the pasta using a colander and reserve 1 cup of the water.

Sauce:

To release its essential oils, toast one teaspoon of freshly cracked pepper for 30 seconds in a large skillet on medium-low heat.

Once the pepper is aromatic, add olive oil and swirl to combine.

When the pasta is almost finished, ladle 4 ounces of the pasta water into the skillet.

Combine:

Add the drained, cooked pasta to the sauce and return the skillet to medium-high heat.

Add half of the Pecorino Romano cheese and continue mixing, adding small amounts of pasta water if the sauce appears dry.

Garnish with the remaining Pecorino Romano and black pepper to taste.

Serve immediately.

Garlic Baked Scallops

Ingredients:

1 pound of large scallops, patted dry

4 tablespoons melted butter or ghee (clarified butter)

3 cloves garlic, minced

1/4 cup breadcrumbs

1/4 cup grated Parmesan cheese

1 tablespoon chopped fresh parsley

1 tablespoon lemon juice

Salt and pepper, to taste

Lemon wedges for serving

Instructions:

Preheat your oven to 400°F

Prepare the garlic butter:

Combine the melted butter, minced garlic, lemon juice, salt, and pepper in a small bowl.

Assemble the scallops:

Arrange the scallops in a single layer in a baking dish.

Drizzle the garlic butter mixture over the scallops, making sure they are thoroughly coated.

Add the topping:

Combine the breadcrumbs, Parmesan cheese, and parsley in a separate small bowl.

Sprinkle this mixture evenly over the scallops.

Bake:

Bake the scallops in a preheated oven for 10 to 12 minutes or until they are opaque and the breadcrumb topping is golden brown.

Serve the baked scallops hot with lemon wedges on the side.

Baked Turkey Meatballs

Whenever I make these meatballs for my grandkids, it always brings big smiles. They're great with or without sauce.

Ingredients:

1 pound 93% lean ground turkey

1/2 teaspoon garlic powder

½ teaspoon dried oregano

1 teaspoon kosher salt

¼ teaspoon ground black pepper

1/3 cup Italian-seasoned breadcrumbs

3 tablespoons finely chopped fresh herbs, basil & parsley,

½ cup grated Parmesan cheese

1 large egg

1 ½ tablespoons extra-virgin olive oil

Instructions:

Preheat your oven to 375°F. Line a rimmed baking sheet with aluminum foil and spray it with nonstick spray (parchment paper can also be used).

Add the cheese, breadcrumbs, herbs, salt, garlic powder, oregano, and pepper in a large mixing bowl and stir well to combine. Add the turkey.

In a small bowl, whisk the egg, then incorporate it into the meat mixture. Using a fork or your fingers, combine until well blended.

Shape the meat into 1-inch meatballs.

Arrange on the prepared baking sheet.

Brush the tops of the meatballs with olive oil.

Bake for 20 minutes or until the meatballs reach an internal temperature of 165°F on an instant-read thermometer.

Sick Day Soup

I make this soup more often than any other dish throughout the year. When I hear that a friend or family member is sick, I immediately pull out my soup pot. You can use frozen turkey meatballs or coarsely shredded chicken from a roasted chicken.

Ingredients:

3 medium carrots, julienne cut (long thin strips, like matchsticks)

3 stalks of celery, julienne cut

1 small onion, chopped

4 cloves garlic, minced

9 cups organic chicken broth (72 ounces)

1 cup dry orzo pasta

2 to 3 handfuls of baby spinach leaves

Salt and pepper to taste

4 cups mini turkey meatballs, half a bag (from the frozen section)

Or 4 cups coarsely shredded chicken (from a roasted chicken)

Grated Parmesan cheese (optional)

Instructions:

Lightly spray a pot with olive oil.

Sauté garlic, onions, carrots, and celery for ten minutes.

Add the broth and bring it to a boil.

Reduce the heat and add the dry pasta. Cover and let it simmer for 10 minutes.

Add the turkey meatballs (or chicken pieces).

Chop baby spinach leaves into large pieces and add to the pot.

Add spinach, salt, and pepper.

Optional: Serve with Parmesan cheese.

Chicken Carbonara

I was invited to a ladies' purse-swap party, where attendees bring their unwanted purses and handbags to trade with others, offering a chance to refresh their collections without spending any money. At the party, I was introduced to this tasty chicken carbonara dish, which I continue to serve at purse swap parties and other ladies' events.

Ingredients:

2 teaspoons olive oil (use less if you add bacon)

4 ounces thinly sliced, chopped pancetta or bacon pieces

2 teaspoons minced garlic

2 ½ cups whipping cream

1 cup freshly grated Parmesan

8 large egg yolks

¼ cup chopped fresh basil leaves

¼ cup chopped fresh Italian parsley leaves

Salt to taste

1 pound of spaghetti

4 cups coarsely shredded chicken (from a roasted chicken)

Black pepper, freshly ground

½ cup chopped walnuts, toasted

1 tablespoon lemon zest

Pasta:

Bring a large pot of salted water to a boil over high heat.

Add the spaghetti and cook for 10 minutes, stirring occasionally, until *al dente*. Drain the pasta.

Pancetta:

Warm the oil in a large skillet over medium heat.

Add the pancetta (or bacon) and garlic, then sauté for approximately 8 minutes until browned and crispy. Set aside to cool.

In a separate large bowl, whisk the cream, cheese, yolks, basil, and parsley until well combined.

Tip: The unused egg whites can be used for a healthy breakfast scramble.

Combine:

Add the chicken and stir to combine it with the pancetta in the same frying pan.

Add the spaghetti and cream mixture, tossing over medium-low heat for about 4 minutes until the chicken is heated and the sauce thickly coats the spaghetti.

Tip: Avoid boiling, as it may scramble the eggs.

Season the pasta with salt and pepper if needed, although the pancetta will likely provide enough salt.

Transfer the pasta to a large, wide serving bowl, and sprinkle it with walnuts and lemon zest.

Serve and enjoy!

Fettuccini Alfredo

I like preparing this recipe for small groups since it is best served from pan to plate.

Ingredients:

12 ounces of fettuccine

4 tablespoons butter (1/2 stick) or ghee (clarified butter)

1 cup heavy cream

1 cup grated Parmesan (4 ounces)

Salt and pepper to taste

Instructions:

Cook fettuccine according to directions.

As the pasta cooks, melt butter in a large skillet over medium-high heat.

Drain the pasta.

Add fettuccine to the skillet with heavy cream, Parmesan, and salt and pepper to taste. Toss over low heat until the pasta is well-coated. Serve immediately.

Slow Cooker Osso Buco

I love using my slow cooker (aka crock pot) for many reasons. The meats turn out so moist and tender, and the delightful aroma fills the house throughout the day. This dish is fragrant and delicious.

Ingredients:

2 tablespoons all-purpose flour

Salt and pepper to taste

6 1-inch-thick slices of veal shank

2 tablespoons butter or ghee (clarified butter)

2 tablespoons olive oil

2 onions, roughly chopped

2 large carrots, chopped

2 stalks of celery, chopped

2 cloves garlic, thinly sliced

1 ¼ cup chicken stock

1 can diced tomatoes (14 ounces)

2 teaspoons chopped fresh oregano

1 bay leaf

Instructions:

Season the flour with salt and pepper.

Toss the veal shank slices with the flour until evenly coated.

Melt the butter and olive oil in a large skillet over medium heat.

Brown the shank slices in the hot butter until golden brown, about 10 minutes per side.

Combine the onions, carrots, celery, and garlic in a large slow cooker.

Set the meat slices atop the vegetables, then pour the chicken stock and diced tomatoes.

Season with oregano and add the bay leaf.

Cook on LOW for 8 hours until the meat falls off the bone.

Season to taste with salt and pepper.

Voilà!

Slow Cooker Chicken Marsala

Ingredients:

6 boneless, skinless chicken breasts (total weight: 1.5 pounds)

1 teaspoon garlic powder

1 teaspoon dried basil

1/2 teaspoon sweet paprika

Salt and freshly ground pepper to your taste.

1 tablespoon olive oil

8 ounces sliced mushrooms

Three cloves garlic, minced

1 cup dry Marsala wine

1/2 cup water

1/4 cup cornstarch

1/4 cup heavy cream

Chopped fresh parsley for garnish.

Tip: opt for dry Marsala wine (sweet Marsala wine is meant for desserts), and steer clear of the cheapest bottles, as they can significantly impact the dish's flavor. If wine isn't your preference, you can use chicken broth instead.

Instructions:

Brown the chicken breasts in a skillet with olive oil for approximately 3 minutes on each side.

Transfer the browned chicken breasts to a 6-quart slow cooker.

Add garlic and sliced mushrooms on top of the chicken breasts.

Deglaze the skillet using Marsala wine, then pour it over the chicken breasts and mushrooms.

Cover and set your slow cooker to LOW for 4 to 5 hours until the chicken is fully cooked. Alternatively, you can cook it on HIGH for 2 to 3 hours.

Remove chicken breasts from the slow cooker and set aside on a plate.

Whisk together water and cornstarch, then add this mixture to the sauce in the slow cooker. Whisk in the heavy cream and return the chicken breasts to the slow cooker.

Check for doneness: Use an instant-read thermometer to determine whether the chicken is cooked. It should reach an internal temperature of 165°F. Approximately 4 to 5 hours on low.

Take your time: Cooking chicken marsala in the crock pot brings a depth of flavor that can only be achieved through low and slow cooking. Don't overlook this advantage!

Eggplant Parmesan

Preparing this dish always reminds me of my sister. It was her favorite dish. She asked me to make it for her when she lost her appetite during her final days. I miss her terribly, but making this dish conjures such sweet memories. Food has a unique way of connecting us to our lost loved ones. That is why sharing recipes is part of how I want to continue my legacy.

Ingredients:

1 large eggplant

1/2 cup olive oil

1/3 cup butter or ghee (clarified butter)

2 eggs

1/4 cup milk

3 cups Italian breadcrumbs

1 cup flour

Tomato sauce, pre-made or store-bought

1 pound mozzarella cheese, grated or thinly sliced

1/2 cup grated Parmesan cheese.

Eggplant:

Peel the eggplant, cutting off the top and bottom.

Slice into 1/8-inch slices and place on large sheets of wax paper.

Tip: Salt the eggplant slices to remove any hint of bitterness. After 10 minutes, turn them over and salt them again. Blot slices dry with a paper towel to remove excess moisture.

The Dredging Station:

Place flour in a shallow bowl.

In a second bowl, whisk two eggs with 1/4 cup milk.

In a third bowl, place 3 cups breadcrumbs.

Dip each piece of eggplant in flour, coating both sides.

Dip each floured slice in egg wash.

Dip slices in breadcrumbs, covering each piece thoroughly.

Instructions:

Preheat the oven to 350 F.

In a large skillet, heat the oil and butter.

Fry the slices in hot oil and butter mixture, browning both sides.

Change the oil/butter mixture to avoid cooking eggplant slices with burnt loose breadcrumbs if necessary.

Place fried eggplant on paper towels to absorb excess oil.

Cover the bottom of your 9x13 baking pan with a thin layer of sauce.

Add a layer of eggplant, top with sauce to cover, and follow with mozzarella and a sprinkle of Parmesan cheese.

Repeat with a second layer, ending with remaining mozzarella and parmesan cheese.

Cover with foil and bake for 20 minutes.

Remove when sauce bubbles and cheese melts.

Serve with a nice salad, garlic bread, and, of course, some wine! I like to serve sorbet for dessert.

The Great Depression Cake

This cake was created during the Depression, 1929-1941. It contains no butter, eggs, or milk, as these ingredients were hard to find at the time. Since many families struggled to get enough food, dessert became a special treat.

Ingredients:

1 ½ cup all-purpose flour

1/3 cup unsweetened cocoa powder

1 cup sugar

1 teaspoon baking soda

1/2 teaspoon kosher salt

1 teaspoon white vinegar

1 teaspoon vanilla extract

1/3 cup vegetable oil

1 cup water

Chocolate frosting of your choice

Instructions:

Preheat oven to 350°F.

Spray a 13x9-inch pan with oil. (I'm sure they used lard back in the day)

Combine the flour, cocoa powder, sugar, baking soda, and salt in the greased pan. Stir gently with a fork or a small whisk to mix.

Make two small wells on the sides and one large well in the center of the dry ingredients. Pour the vinegar and vanilla into the small wells, then add the oil to the large well; if it spills over, that's fine. Pour the water on top and whisk again to combine thoroughly.

Bake for 30 to 35 minutes or until a toothpick inserted in the center comes out clean. Let it cool completely.

Frost the cake with chocolate frosting.

Optional: sprinkles on top.   Enjoy!

Store:

Once the cake has cooled, you can freeze it whole or in individual slices. You may freeze the cake frosted or unfrosted. If you freeze the cake with frosting, place it on a plate before wrapping. This helps prevent the frosting from sticking to the wrap.

We always save the best for last...

Mom's Cheesecake

<u>Ingredients</u>

1/2 teaspoon salt

1 teaspoon vanilla

¾ cup sugar

three 8-ounce packages of cream cheese

4 egg whites

A large store-bought graham cracker crust pie pan is ideal (or you can buy a box of graham cracker crumbs and make your own).

<u>Instructions</u>

Beat egg whites to a peak, and slowly add sugar, salt, vanilla, and cream cheese.

<u>For a store-bought pre-made graham cracker crust</u>

Pour the cream cheese mixture into a large store-bought graham cracker crust pie pan.

Bake at 350°F for 25 minutes.

Cool overnight in the fridge.

<u>For homemade graham cracker crust</u>

1-1/2 cups crushed graham cracker crumbs

1/4 cup sugar

1/3 cup butter, melted

A sprinkle of cinnamon

Pour the crust into the pie pan and press down firmly using a second pie pan on top. Remove the top pie pan, add the cream cheese mixture and bake.

Bake at 350°F for 25 minutes.

Cool overnight in the fridge.

Cooking Tips and Tricks

Selecting the right pan is essential for the success of your dish. Stainless steel is best for delicate foods like vegetables and fish. Cast iron is excellent for high-heat dishes, while nonstick pans are perfect for low-heat foods such as pancakes and omelets. To alleviate stress while cooking, it's important to gather your ingredients ahead of time. Prepare your vegetables, measure your spices, and marinate your meats before cooking.

To determine if your heated oil is hot enough for frying, dip the end of a wooden spoon into it. If you observe tiny bubbles forming, the oil is ready. Alternatively, you can add a few pieces of onion or a small splash of water. If you hear that delightful sizzle, you're all set. Adding food to oil that isn't hot enough will create a soggy mess. If you overheat your oil, it will start to smoke. Not only does this smell and taste bad, but it also poses a fire risk. It's best to test!

A 7-inch carrot contains over 5 grams of sugar. When simmered in sauce, this root vegetable not only adds sweetness but also balances the acidity of the tomatoes.

Always store cooked *al dente* pasta in the refrigerator. This makes it easy to prepare a delicious dinner quickly.

Remember, pasta water can help a sauce come together, so when you drain your pasta, always save a cup or two. You can keep some pasta water in the fridge for reheating leftovers. In fact, you can use pasta water, stock, or even plain water. Reheat it and add a bit of the liquid to your food. It might need a little salt or a touch of cheese. Then bring it back to eating temperature. It's good. I love reheated pasta.

I enjoy having a fresh salad with my dinner. To keep it crisp, I buy a whole head of green leaf lettuce or spinach (not pre-packaged), rinse it, pat it dry with a paper towel, and store it in the refrigerator. This allows me to mix the desired amount with freshly cut tomatoes and cucumbers. Occasionally, I enhance my salad with avocados, kalamata olives, and feta or blue cheese crumbles as toppings. I recommend using Marston's San Pasqual dressing, which is usually available at Bashas' and AJ's stores in Arizona, or you can order it online. This dressing has a flavor similar to the Italian dressing I make from scratch. Moreover, it's gluten-free and made with all-natural ingredients.

With these simple tips and recipes, I hope you enjoy preparing, sharing, and savoring delicious foods that nourish the body and spirit.

Bon appétit! Or, considering the Italian menu, MANGIA!

Chapter 6 - Voices From The Ones Left Behind

Sharing stories is important. Stories help us heal and support others coping with their emotional grief. It's vital for grieving people to realize they are not alone on their journey. When I started writing this book, I was transported back in time, reliving every detail, which was quite emotional. Sometimes, I had to set my writing aside and come back to it weeks later. Including anecdotes about the funny experiences my three husbands and I shared was helpful and therapeutic for me.

In this chapter, you'll hear heartfelt stories from widows and widowers about how they coped and moved forward. I hope you find these accounts both helpful and enjoyable. Some may surprise you. The first one might seem harsh and not promote healing, but it actually has the opposite effect. Acknowledging and examining our inner thoughts and feelings can be a powerful tool for personal growth.

One contributor, Carey Conley, shares her story from her book, *Keep Looking Up,* which recounts how she and her daughter found purpose and hope after both her husband and son took their own lives. Victoria Benoit describes her unique Celebration of Life event in her inspiring book *No Weeping Widow Here: My True Story.*

Regardless of who the contributor is, even if some choose to remain anonymous, you'll find innovative ideas that inspire you to let joy brighten the darker corners of your heart.

Annie from Sun City, Arizona

I'm glad he's dead. A strong sense of renewal flows through me. Since my husband's death, I've experienced a deep sense of freedom I never expected. Surprisingly, I have no regrets about our life together or his passing; in fact, I realize I don't miss him at all. It's amazing to see how my happiness has increased since he left. For the first time, I'm embracing my own worth and recognizing the strength inside me. I no longer see myself as inadequate, but instead see the potential for joy and fulfillment ahead. This newfound clarity enables me to pursue my dreams and discover what truly brings me happiness, free from the shadows of the past.

Kelly Menefee Miller Looks to the Future

A strong, healthy relationship with family, friends, and God helped me the most. Grief counseling provided through my church enhanced the healing process. It's hard to step outside your comfort zone and talk to strangers about your bleeding heart. Yet, it helped, and knowing the "you are not alone" part is crucial.

Sometimes, it's okay to say, "There's nothing good about today," because it reflects a real feeling or truth. We've all feared the night and dreaded the dawn. Keep busy and look ahead, as we are still here on this earth for a reason.

Carey Conley Promotes Vision and Purpose – When Life Isn't What You Envisioned Part 1

Last week was my husband Ross's 61st birthday. It isn't easy to believe he has been gone for almost eight years. When milestone days like this creep up, it gives me pause to reflect on the way I envisioned my life before losing Ross and later losing my son to suicide.

Ross and I had a high school romance and married soon after graduating college. We had a good 35 years together. When I said, "I do," I thought we would grow old together. Never in a million years did I envision myself as a single mother, much less a single grandmother. Two years before Ross passed away, we downsized into what I thought would be our family home, where the kids would visit with their own families. We remodeled the basement to ensure plenty of room for holiday visits, vacation times, etc. It was a beautiful plan.

Many people who have faced similar unimaginable adversities tend to shy away from envisioning and writing out what they want their future to look like. It would be easy to say, "With so many things outside of my control, why bother?"

One of my favorite quotes is by Andy Stanley: "Pencil in your plans but write your vision in ink." I believe your vision (the strong desires of your heart and soul) exists because when you follow it, your purpose is revealed. God did not place those yearnings in your heart by accident. I believe they call out to you because they are revealing your purpose and identity. Even with all the changes in my life, my purpose has not changed. As a matter of fact, these circumstances have only served to fuel my purpose.

Writing your plans (actions) in pencil allows you to change course when the unexpected happens. Even though my family dynamic has changed drastically and is not how I envisioned it, I still follow my purpose daily. I take time to absorb the changes, give myself time and space to grieve, and surround myself with people who love and believe in me.

I know God prepared me for this time when I wrote out my first life vision over 30 years ago. He knew what was coming. For all those years of being anchored in my vision, and helping hundreds of people write out their own, I have built a rock-solid foundation for carrying out my present mission.

"Dissolve to Evolve" - part 2 – Carey Conley

A new friend of mine posted this phrase on Instagram the other day, and it resonated with me. In multiple ways, this has been my life for almost ten years. It's a painful but necessary process to be who God intended us to be and carry out our purpose.

Our childhood relationships and education often create a false identity. Unless we take the time to become aware and do the internal work to follow our own truth, most of us die feeling unfulfilled and with many regrets. So sad.

Choosing to know who you are and what you are uniquely called to do requires dissolving: the act of dispersing, disappearing, or bringing something to an end. Here are some areas I have had to dissolve to evolve:

- My physical space. Since 2012, I have moved multiple times. I began in a 6,000-square-foot home and now reside in a 1,100-square-foot apartment. It is impossible to say how many things I let go of with each move. Most of this had to do with losing my husband and son, but people should start purging long before their family members must do it for them. It's only stuff, but it can be such a weight.

- My relationships. I believe most people we allow in are only there for a season. Every year, I evaluate my "front row" and decide how to bless and release people who will not help me keep growing. This front row gets smaller as I get older.

- The DOING. This year, I made a choice to stop doing things just because they are what I have always done or because of the need to prove myself to others and myself. The time has come to question my identity and get rock solid on my purpose and how to use my knowledge and experience to be of service. Having so much space in my life is super uncomfortable, but the messages from God, my loving daughter, and my mentors were precise. It was time for me to learn to love, wait for God's best for me, and enjoy the ride!

- Old stuff. This includes dissolving old patterns, habits, self-care, and self-talk that are not the best. I read that if we talked to our friends the way we talk to ourselves sometimes, we wouldn't have any. I am spending more time expanding my loving, empowering thoughts through prayer, reading scripture, and journaling affirmations daily.

I crave evolution. I want to live a more joyful, purposeful, and authentic life for myself, my family, and all of you. I am confident my purpose is to help people get clear on who they are, move through the dissolving to evolving process, and create the life of their dreams. If you are thinking about it and feeling it in your heart, it means it is already there for you.

Cheers to evolving!

Still Alive but Dead to Me – Micheal Smith

My wife is still alive, but the person I once knew is gone. Dementia took her mind over two years ago. For over a year now, she has looked at me with no recognition in her eyes.

In the beginning, there were still moments of clarity—precious days when laughter helped bridge the growing gap between us as we revisited memories of our life together. I remember the day we christened our new espresso machine. I had carefully studied the manual, eager for that first perfect cup. However, when I pressed the start button, it erupted like a caffeinated volcano, with coffee spraying across the walls and ceiling in an impressive display of brewing gone wrong. I stood there stunned, coffee dripping from my face and arms, thoroughly soaked and sticky.

She laughed until tears streamed down her face. Her happiness was so genuine and contagious that, despite my coffee-soaked state, I couldn't resist joining her in laughter.

Those moments are gone now. How do you look into the eyes of someone you've loved for decades, only to see a stranger staring back? The deep unfairness of it weighs heavily—this living loss where the physical form remains but the essence of the person you cherished has slipped away, leaving only echoes of what once was.

Candace's Letter to Bobbie – Candace Stillman

I am a nurse with years of experience in hospice care, as well as personal experience with loss. Everyone takes a different path toward healing, but generally, the first three months bring shock, followed by the next three months when the shock begins to fade.

For me, the first six months felt like living through a horrible nightmare I couldn't wake up from. Sleep was hard to find, and it was such a relief to escape the unbearable pain whenever I could finally sleep. Sometimes, I felt like I was losing my mind.

The point is to be patient and kind to yourself. I share your philosophy, Bobbie, that life experiences help us grow stronger. I promise you that one day, you will stop feeling that unbearable pain.

Bobbie, you said your husband is your special angel watching over you. That will probably grow into a deeper connection with him than ever before, though you will always miss his physical presence.

From One Old Guy

Alright, here it goes. I'm old. That means I've survived, and many of the people I've known and loved are no longer here. I've lost friends, best friends, acquaintances, co-workers, grandparents, my mom, relatives, teachers, mentors, students, neighbors, and others. I have no children, and I can't imagine the pain of losing a child. But here are my two cents.

I wish I could say you get used to people dying, but I never did, and I don't want to. It tears a hole through me whenever someone I love dies, regardless of the circumstances. But I don't want it to "not matter." I don't want it to be something that just passes. My scars are a testament to my love and relationship with that person. If the scar is deep, so is the love. So be it.

Scars are a symbol of life. They demonstrate that I can love deeply, live fully, endure wounds or even gouges, and still heal to keep on living and loving. Additionally, the scar tissue is stronger than the original flesh ever was.

Grief hits in waves. When the ship sinks, you're left drowning among wreckage. Every piece that floats nearby reminds you of the ship's former beauty and grandeur, now lost. All you can do is stay afloat. Stay alive.

You find some wreckage and hold onto it for a while. It might be a physical object, a joyful memory, or a photograph. It could even be another person who is also floating.

In the beginning, the waves are 100 feet tall and crash over you without mercy. They come every 10 seconds and don't let you catch your breath. All you can do is hang on and float. After a while—maybe weeks, maybe months—you'll find that the waves are still 100 feet tall, but they come further apart. When they come, they still crash over you and wipe you out. But in between, you can breathe. You can function. You never know what will trigger grief. It might be a song, a picture, a street intersection, or the smell of a cup of coffee. It can be just about anything... and then the wave comes crashing. But in between waves, there is life.

Somewhere along the way, which varies for everyone, the waves are only 80 or 50 feet tall. While they still arrive, they come less often. You can see them approaching on an anniversary, a birthday, Christmas, or when landing at a familiar airport. You recognize the waves coming, and for the most part, you prepare yourself. When they wash over you, you somehow know you will emerge on the other side. Soaking wet, sputtering, still holding on to a small piece of the wreckage, but you'll get through.

Take it from an old guy: the waves never stop coming, and somehow, you don't want them to. But you learn to survive all the waves that come. You'll survive those, too. You'll have many scars from love and shipwrecks if you're lucky.

Gabby Says Don't Wait

I was recently with a woman who said goodbye to her husband just hours before she died. She whispered, "Thank you for loving me." He replied, "You are easy to love."

Tears streamed so quickly from my eyes down my cheeks that I couldn't hold them back. This couple spent 30 years together, reminding each other of their love, so when it was time to say goodbye, all they needed to say was, "Thank you."

I want to live with the people I love and who love me, where we don't have to prove our feelings because we already know. When we say goodbye, we carry that unconditional love with us. What a gift.

Let's remind the people in our lives how much we love them. Don't wait until it's too late to express everything, make up for lost time, or wish you had more time. Make the most of your time now so that when you have to say goodbye, you only need to say, "Thank you for loving me."

David Rebuilds a Life

My partner and I lived a very private life together for nine years. It was almost like living a double life in some ways. While Joseph was comfortable sharing our relationship with others, I preferred to keep it within our immediate circle of friends. I was not ashamed of my homosexuality, but fear held me back from revealing my true identity. I worried that my legal practice would suffer and my credibility at the law firm would be damaged. It wasn't until I lost Joseph, the one person in my life who brought me joy and happiness, that I realized how mistaken I had been. Joseph lost his life in a tragic accident caused by a drunk driver.

I was afraid to join a grief group because I thought I wouldn't fit in. For months, I struggled with the pain of losing the one person who loved me unconditionally. A friend suggested that I take a ten-day cruise for gay singles. After careful consideration, I chose to go.

Throughout the trip, I felt comfortable around different groups of people: confident men and women, some bold and flamboyant, while others were more reserved and conservative. Everyone proudly embraced their unique lifestyle choices, creating an atmosphere of acceptance and support. I eagerly participated in various engaging activities, immersing myself in classes led by captivating speakers whose ideas sparked my curiosity and inspiration. It was comforting to know I had company, and I grew stronger each day. When I got back home, I felt more self-assured and was determined to continue building a social life. My personal life choices will stay private, but I am now more open to joining like-minded groups and events that will help me grow.

Hubby Dies During Covid

My husband's last year was the most difficult in our 52 years of marriage. His behavior was rude and unpleasant. I now realize this was mainly caused by the repeated brain bleeds we didn't know about. Even his best friend noticed a sharp change in his personality.

I hated living alone, so I put the house on the market within a week of his death. I got rid of many reminders and downsized everything. After spending a long time on the market, the house sold at a loss, but by then, I didn't care. I had already planned my move to an independent living facility in Colorado so I could be close to my son without being too close. He calls me almost every day, and I see him often. I am content with my life, but sometimes I miss my husband terribly.

Because of Covid and hospital rules, I couldn't be there when he died. He had a massive stroke and never woke up again. All I felt was a deep relief that his pain had ended. Life doesn't always have a fairy tale ending.

My Choice This Time

In some cultures, arranged marriages are common. In these cases, parents or other family members select a spouse for their child. This is not considered a forced marriage, and mutual affection often develops between the bride and groom. Instead of making a quick decision based on passion or lust, couples who marry through an arrangement can fall just as deeply in love as those who meet by chance. Arranged marriages can offer financial stability, cultural similarities between partners, stronger family ties, and shared values. However, love is often not a factor in the arrangement.

Furthermore, arranged marriages eliminate the dating stage of life. It's important to understand that in some cultures, going against the arrangement can result in disownment and exile from the family. Arranged marriages remain common in India.

At just seventeen, I entered into an arranged marriage with my new husband, who was twenty. After moving to the United States, we kept our family traditions. We lived in a beautiful home in a fancy neighborhood and raised two children. From an outsider's view, our life seemed better than average and even enviable to some. However, no one could understand the deep emptiness I felt inside. In my culture, it's customary for a wife to stand behind her husband and follow his lead. For twenty-two years, I followed this tradition.

After my husband's death, a new chapter in my life began. Now that I am a widow, I feel empowered to live on my own terms and make my own choices. For the first time in a long while, I feel a sense of freedom and independence. Setting my own boundaries and choosing the path I want to follow has been truly empowering.

Stephen Wu's Journey – Life as We Know It Ends- part 1

On December 20, 2019, we left our home in Chandler, Arizona, in the mid-morning and began our long-awaited road trip to Death Valley National Park. My wife and I enjoyed traveling together, taking in the natural beauty across the country. We explored 40 states and over 20 national parks. We chose to take our new sedan instead of her larger minivan because my daughter had just received her license and wanted to drive some during the vacation.

We were just a few miles from the park after a seven-hour drive and a restroom break at the Hoover Dam. It was shortly after sunset, during twilight. I was driving on a winding two-lane road, ascending a moderate hill, when a car suddenly appeared, heading straight towards me. It was attempting to pass another vehicle in a no-passing zone. In what felt like the slowest second of my life, both cars tried to avoid each other, but it was too late. I felt the explosive impact of the collision as my car screeched to a halt sideways. The other vehicle disappeared into a dark ditch off-road.

I didn't know how I found the strength to open the door, but I managed to help my daughter and son out. I went to the backseat and saw my wife sitting there. She had apparently lost consciousness. Her side of the car was relatively unscathed, so I felt somewhat reassured that she would be okay. I left her resting inside while I frantically searched for help.

Several bystanders stopped to help us and attempted to call 911 despite having very poor cell signals. It took 45 minutes for the first police patrol to arrive, followed by additional medics. A female medic checked on my wife twice and asked me to cover her with an extra jacket for warmth. The medic helicopter arrived an hour and a half after the collision. The medic approached me, lowered her gaze, and delivered the unimaginable news, "I am sorry, but she didn't make it." I remember our desperate cry that cold night, "NO!"

The following days and weeks were a blur. We were taken to the Las Vegas trauma center. My daughter and I, both suffering from severe internal injuries, received treatment in the ICU for nine days. Afterward, we were discharged and returned home for an additional three months of recovery with home care. My mother-in-law and sister-in-law flew in from Shanghai, China, for the funeral service, which nearly two hundred of our friends, colleagues, classmates, and neighbors attended. Twenty of my daughter's high school classmates came to support her. The outpouring of love was overwhelming.

Stephen Wu's Journey continues – Trigger Dates-part 2

The past week and a half have been busy with "trigger dates" and events: my wife and son's joint birthdays (my wife had a C-section, so our son's birth was planned for her birthday), then Mother's Day, my son's prom, his graduation, and my birthday. It's been an emotional marathon, but I surprised myself by not crying.

Not a day has gone by in the last 29 months that I haven't missed my wife, and I have maintained my new habit of writing to her in my journal every night. I believe I have reached the much-coveted yet often misunderstood final stage of grieving—acceptance. I recognize that acceptance involves embracing all facets of life, including the ebbs and flows of my emotions. Yin and yang, joy, and sadness are at peace with each other and allow space for coexistence.

Stephen Wu's Journey continues – 28.5 Years of Marriage-part 3

I promised to spend one last memorable summer with my children before they head off to college. My son is entering his freshman year, and my daughter is starting her sophomore year. We had just returned from our first trip to Europe, where we visited Germany and Austria, places my wife had been to two decades ago. The kids and I are at home resting for a couple of weeks before we leave for Hawaii to celebrate our 30th wedding anniversary. Travel has always been our passion since we met and fell in love, and it has shaped a significant part of our life together. It is also a vital component in my healing recipe. With each trip, I feel like I'm bringing her along with me, creating new memories together in spirit.

The defining moment of our romance occurred during a road trip. We were both graduate students at the University of Virginia and met at a game night at a mutual friend's apartment. Through introductions, we discovered that our family homes in China were just 20 minutes apart in the same city. While it wasn't a love-at-first-sight story, we became friends and enjoyed each other's company. As summer arrived, most of our friends worked with professors on research projects during the break, but we decided to drive to Niagara Falls. On a drizzly morning near the Falls, our car was rear-ended by friends following us. Upon impact, I instinctively grabbed her hand. Our eyes met, and sparks flew. The rest is history.

We got married in the famous historic school chapel exactly a year after the incident.

Our twenty-eight and a half years of marriage had its share of trials. Our first child suffered from an inherited degenerative disorder and passed away as a toddler. Two years later, my wife experienced a miscarriage. Fortunately, we welcomed a healthy boy shortly after and adopted a beautiful girl from abroad. We relocated for work three times across the country. My wife was a successful professional in the financial industry, on the fast track to becoming a senior manager.

In addition to our busy careers, we enjoyed outdoor activities, movies, and social gatherings. She became a quick learner in the arts and created several wonderful paintings, but our top passion was traveling. Our trips brought us closer as a couple and as a family once we had kids.

How did I cope with my grief and move forward to heal? Gratitude, resilience, social engagement, and a sense of responsibility played a crucial role in my journey. I needed all the support I could find, and thankfully, I received more than enough. Online communities for widows and widowers, in-person group meetings, grief self-help books, counselors, friends, colleagues, and family all contributed. Self-discovery and self-awareness also aided me in resetting my expectations.

Stephen Wu's Journey continues - On Again, Off Again-part 4

Like fingerprints, our journeys are distinctive to our personalities, the nature and depth of our relationships, and the circumstances of their passage.

"Healing" is attributed to many factors. I feel mostly upbeat and happy with my life right now, and in many ways, I am better than ever. However, the grieving ghost has never completely vanished. Yesterday, I treated myself to the movie *Elvis* and silently wept in the back row during "Can't Help Falling in Love." I can't shake it from my mind, and my eyes have been misty for most of the day.

I am in the final stage of grieving, which is acceptance. I embrace my emotions as they arise and acknowledge the enduring duality of feeling glad and sad either simultaneously or alternately. I can build a new life filled with excitement and fulfillment while keeping her in my heart.

I have always been resilient, and resilience has aided my recovery from the depths of sorrow. For example, there was a time I found myself at the bottom of the Grand Canyon during a rim-to-rim hike a year before the accident. It was dark and cold, and I was nearly exhausted. The only thing that propelled me forward was the mantra of taking one more step, which I repeated until I reached the top. I shared that story with my children as I held them close on the night of the accident. We have been moving forward one step at a time for the last thirty months and ten days.

My dear mother-in-law, upon hearing the devastating news, reminded me of my parental responsibility to stay alive: "You have to be strong. Otherwise, they will be orphans." That was a powerful reminder to care for something bigger than myself.

Gratitude is a powerful healing potion. I owe my very survival, both physically and emotionally, to the help and support of countless individuals. First, I cannot thank the medical professionals enough for saving the lives of my children and me. Among my most precious memories is a family of strangers who pulled over after the accident and offered us the chance to lie on the heated seats of their truck while letting their young children stand in the cold. I remember two ICU nurses who spent their break chatting with me, providing comfort.

Several volunteers from local Asian churches near our hospital in Las Vegas visited me, bringing food and snacks. Nearly 80 volunteers from the local Asian community in Phoenix formed makeshift groups to provide homemade meals. Their selfless acts filled me with hope for humanity and encouraged me to appreciate life even when times are tough.

Stephen Wu's Journey continues – Intellection-part 5

Years ago, at my company, our HR encouraged employees to take a Strengths Finder assessment. One of my top personality strengths was identified as *intellection*, which is the deep intellectual pursuit of meaning and understanding. This is no surprise, as I grew up in a family of college educators. When I began the grieving process, a couple of friends gave me self-help books on coping with grief, and I absorbed them wholeheartedly. The book that profoundly influenced me was *Option B* by Facebook COO Sheryl Sandberg, who lost her husband to a sudden, unexpected illness. I was moved by her brutal transparency about her own long healing journey, along with her unquenchable empathy and relatability with others who suffer from personal traumas of all kinds.

I learned about the three Ps of early grieving: personalization ("it's all my fault"), pervasiveness ("everything in the world sucks"), and permanence ("I will be miserable forever"). I can completely relate to each one. But more importantly, I found that there is hope for "post-traumatic growth."

People may have different motivations for post-traumatic growth. Mine is to live in a way that would make my wife proud of me. Throughout our 29 years together, she proved to be a better person than I am: smarter, kinder, far more successful in her career, and a superior parent. After her passing, I spent a long time reflecting on the past and was deeply appalled by my many flaws. I wish I could have been different then, but I am determined to live the remainder of my life as a better person in her honor.

My manager once joked that, like her daughter, I have a "helping gene" that generates energy through helping others. At least it helps divert attention away from the "miserable me." It all starts at home. Before the accident, I was too consumed with my own career to pay attention to my kids. Afterward, I was determined to change that by bonding with them and assisting with their home-work and college preparations. I take pride in the fact that both my children have graduated from high school and have been accepted into the colleges of their choice. I hope their mom is happy.

As I mentioned, I joined several online communities for widows and widowers to seek support. Sharing the same pain and healing has helped me immensely. I also contribute as much as I can to assist others. I find that my efforts are therapeutic for me as well. I have always enjoyed volunteering with charities and nonprofit organizations. Over the last two years, I have become a board member of two nonprofits. Knowing my efforts are valuable helps to ease my own sorrows.

Stephen Wu's Journey continues – Anniversary Blues - part 6

Today is tough; it's our 30th anniversary. I went to a spectacular viewpoint on the hotel grounds overlooking a beautiful beach and laid flowers on an empty chair. I listened to Elvis's "I Can't Help Falling in Love" and had a good cry.

Stephen Wu's Journey continues – The Divine Arrangement-part 7

Today, I went to Prescott and joined a few other widows and widowers for a hiking picnic. As if by divine arrangement, we were all in the same age group, and our losses were similarly tragic and unexpected. We felt an instant camaraderie, bonding through story sharing and laughter. It was very therapeutic. I guess this leads to another central theme of my healing: socialization.

I am an only child in my family. Much of my childhood and youth was spent in solitude. I consider myself an introvert, and I was tested as such early in my career. However, as my career progressed, I became more socially engaged. After the accident, I instinctively leaned on my social circles for support. When the pandemic forced a lockdown, restricting in-person contact just as I began my grieving process, I hosted several Zoom meetings. I invited friends from high school and college to my old neighborhood in North Carolina and kept in touch with some of my wife's friends.

Although a thousand friends could never replace the deep intimacy my wife and I shared, social networking has directed my attention outward to others and has alleviated my loneliness and depression. In short, socialization allows me to be part of a larger world that deserves care and offers compassion in return.

Interestingly, my disciplined analytical thinking and strategic mindset played a minor yet noteworthy role in my recovery. Amid the chaos of the early days, I was able to compile a list of all the urgent, essential tasks, prioritize them by relevance, and create action plans. These professional habits helped preserve my sanity as I managed our finances, supported my two teens with their schoolwork and extracurricular activities, cared for my parents and in-laws, and handled my own work.

Stephen Wu's Journey continues – A Spiritual Journey-part 8

I saved the hardest subject for last: spirituality, which is crucial for grief recovery.

The pandemic was difficult for me. After a three-month medical leave, I returned to work for half a week before we were asked to work from home. Before that, my in-laws had flown in from Shanghai to attend the funeral. They returned on the eve of the mandatory quarantine issued by the Chinese government. It was heartbreaking not to be there with them and comfort them when they needed support. The silver lining is that we grew closer. We video-chatted weekly, whereas before, I hardly ever spoke to them. Maintaining communication has been healing for all of us.

Spirituality serves as our invisible compass in life. It encompasses our deep-rooted beliefs, hopes, and rationales about the world, transcending our normal perception of reality. There is nothing quite like personal trauma to shake a person's belief system.

When I arrived home from the funeral, my home health nurse pointed out the vibrant yellow rose in full bloom in my front courtyard. I froze. The yellow rose was my wife's favorite. My nurse and I shared a knowing look and nodded in agreement: she's still here, and that's her sign!

I never believed in psychics before and considered them to be borderline con artists. After her passing, I decided to see two psychics out of curiosity. At the very least, I approached these sessions as a form of alternative counseling and life coaching. I left feeling even more convinced of the inconclusiveness of it all. Some aspects of the readings were surprisingly genuine, while others seemed sketchier.

As I delved deeper into my philosophical contemplation, I accepted two basic principles: spiritual pursuit and cognitive ability.

First, the only logical explanation concerning the afterlife is that it is unknowable. This remains true despite the earnest attempts of religion, philosophy, and science to loosen the grip of the unknown. With all the incredible power of human imagination and ingenuity, we know only an infinitesimal fraction of the universe. Accepting that there is much that is unknown, or perhaps unknowable, during our lifetime brings me peace of mind.

Secondly, the fable of the Blind Men and the Elephant may best capture the essence of human spirituality. It's quite possible that those with long-held competing beliefs—such as religions, folk traditions, philosophers, gurus, and scientists—each grasp some kernels of truth, much like each blind man accurately understood parts of the elephant in the tale. We stand to gain a lot by staying open-minded. With these two realizations in mind, I have become less anxious over the last two years.

Stephen Wu's Journey continues – 31 Months Later - part 9

I've read that the emotion most harmful to health is guilt. After the accident, I was overwhelmed by guilt. First, countless should-have/could-have scenarios have prevented the tragedy. We should have driven my wife's larger van instead of my sedan. I should have started driving earlier, and I should not have stopped for a restroom break, but it went on and on. My counselor helped me to stop over-analyzing the chance-driven incident. Even my daughter offered a thoughtful perspective: "Dad, it's not YOUR fault; it's the fault of that other driver! Stop blaming yourself for it."

But there is a darker, deeper level of guilt and shame that has haunted me. To others, we had a beautiful marriage and enviable careers, but I had made my fair share of mistakes and, at times, did not treat her as well as she deserved. Although we maintained our love through the ups and downs, I was appalled by my flaws. I fantasized that God took her away because I didn't deserve such pure, unconditional love. My counselor told me, "The fact that she continued to love you means you are better than you think; there must be something good in you that deserved her love."

A different kind of self-talk ultimately saved me from despair. I still don't understand why I survived this tragedy while she did not. Perhaps there is a divine purpose for me to remain on this earth. This motivates me to live each day as a better person. I may have let her down before, but I will not let her down as long as I live.

Not a moment has passed in the last thirty-one months that I haven't wished to turn back time and bring her back. Yet, as much as I grieve and would gladly switch places with her, I remind myself to keep living a life that would make her proud.

Marcia's Two Richies

Richie and I lived in the same apartment building in Queens, New York, and met in the laundry room. He was 26, and I was 38, and we hit it off right away. Richie was the most wonderful person I have ever met, and this remains true today. Due to the age difference, people doubted that our love would last. We sure proved them wrong!

Richie told me right off he had a congenital heart condition and had suffered a heart attack at 19, but I loved him so much I didn't care. We got married on December 3, 1977.

Richie experienced several heart attacks and underwent bypass surgery. We were constantly traveling from Scottsdale to Tucson for medical procedures. Ultimately, he required a heart transplant. When they called to say they had a heart for him, we sang, "We're off to see the wizard, the wonderful Wizard of Oz" as we hit the road to Tucson. Our hopes were high, and so were we!

Nine years later, Richie lost his battle with heart disease. He was 53, and I was 65. We had been together for 27 years. The grieving period was lengthy, and coping was challenging. Besides being the perfect partner, Richie did everything for me. He filled my car with gas, helped me clean the house, and made me feel like a princess.

Nights without Richie were terrible. Thank goodness I had our dog, Buddy, to keep me company that first year. I also had many friends who encouraged me to get out of the house and made me laugh. Daily walks through the neighborhood with dog treats in my pocket brought me joy. All those wagging tails and wet kisses comforted my aching heart.

A year later, I sold our house on 96th Street and bought a smaller home near 110th, choosing to remain close by. Even the smaller house seemed big. I decided to get another pet, and I chose a cat, not just any cat, but a Rag Doll with personality plus. I named him RJ for Richie Junior. RJ was as fantastic a cat as Richie was a man.

RJ lived for 17 ½ years, but when he died, I felt like I was losing Richie all over again. At 86, I understand that grief fades but still comes in waves. Yes, we move on (I have a new cat, Gracie), and we go on with our lives, but it can still hurt because, unlike grief, true love never fades, and love is worth the pain.

Lari's Path to Inspiration – Happiness is a Decision - part 1

My name is Laraine (Lari). My husband was Roger Yasui, and our children are Yvette, born in 1966, and Ryan, born in 1968.

This is the story about Roger's death.

Sunday, July 12, 2015, was a hot and muggy day. It was 13 days before our 50th anniversary party at the Natsu Noya Tea House in Honolulu. At 2 pm, I got ready to leave for my taiko (drumming) class. Roger said, "When you get home, let's go to Costco because I need bread, and then let's go to dinner." I agreed and left. Two hours later, when I returned, I couldn't find Roger anywhere.

After searching the house, I checked in front of the garage. From the patio, I investigated the backyard—no sign of Roger. I turned the corner behind our bedroom and found him lying on the grass with a dirt-filled shovel and his slippers nearby.

I screamed hysterically, and the neighbors rushed over to perform CPR on Roger. We called 911, and I reached out to my son, Ryan. A fire truck, an ambulance, the police, and Ryan all arrived. The EMTs worked on him, placed him on a gurney, and loaded him into the ambulance. I told them, "He doesn't want to be resuscitated." After a few minutes of treatment in the ambulance, they said they were taking him to Pali Momi Medical Center.

Ryan drove me there. I guessed that Roger, who was in the air-conditioned family room watching TV, decided to do some yard work shortly after I left home. We waited in a room until a female doctor and a male nurse entered with somber expressions and informed us that Roger couldn't be saved. The doctor said they would clean him up, allowing us to stay with him for four hours. They brought him to the chapel, where immediate family and close friends gathered.

Roger appeared peaceful and felt lifelike to the touch, as if he were simply sleeping. We gathered at his side, shared prayers, and reminisced together until it was time for the staff to take his body away. We all embraced him and said our goodbyes.

That night, Legacy of Life called about organ and tissue donation. I spent an hour on the phone with them, answering their medical questions. Even in my grief, I was more than willing to help with any organ or tissue transplant.

I found the paper Roger wrote about his funeral wishes years ago when I took Dr. Mitsuo Aoki's Death and Dying course at the University of Hawaii. That made it easier to follow Roger's wishes. He specified that he wanted to be cremated and to have a short, simple service—nothing fancy—with refreshments served to guests—something to "my wife's liking," as he put it.

The next day, I called several relatives and friends to inform them of Roger's death. My daughter, Yvette, pleaded with me to allow her to help with the arrangements. I explained that we needed to find a large church for the service because the mortuary was fully booked for a month. I suggested she start with Kalihi Union Church. Fortunately, there were dates available soon after our anniversary party was scheduled.

I asked Yvette and Ryan what they would like to do with Roger's ashes: bury him at Punchbowl National Cemetery or scatter them. Both expressed a preference for scattering them. Initially, I wasn't sure where to do it, but someone mentioned that Roger had spent his childhood in Ewa Beach, and I agreed it was the perfect place.

Ryan took the whole week off work to accompany me to all my appointments. After my doctor's visit, we stopped by the church to meet with the pastor. We set the date and time for the memorial service on July 28, three days after the upcoming anniversary party. We also visited the mortuary and consulted our financial advisor, who was a close friend and like a brother to Roger. We finalized the obituary, determined how many copies of the death certificate to request, and decided when to view the body before cremation.

I was devastated that Roger had died just before our 50th anniversary party. Yvette mentioned that it would be like him to go right before the party. That way, no one would have to make a special trip for his service. Forty-five people had already made plans to come from Kona, Japan, and the mainland. Two hundred family and friends had RSVP'd to attend the anniversary party. I did not have the heart to cancel the event. Roger would not have wanted me to cancel.

Rather than celebrating our anniversary, we transformed it into a celebration of Roger. I hired a photographer and a musician, and we ordered desserts. Many people offered to assist with Roger's Celebration of Life event and the memorial service at the church. Receiving so much love and support from family and friends was a true blessing.

At the memorial service, our grandchildren all spoke about a special memory of their grandpa. Then, we had an open mic for guests to share something about Roger, and many of them shared funny stories. It was so memorable.

Several other friends mentioned they had stories about Roger but hesitated to share them. This sparked an idea in me. I reached out to as many friends and family members as I could and asked them to send me a story about Roger. I compiled all the stories into a memory book on Shutterfly. Ryan and Yvette's families each received a copy, and the grandkids will always have Grandpa Roger's stories to read and cherish.

About 800 people attended the memorial service, and around 600 stayed to eat. The reception was held in the gym, and even former Governor Ben Cayetano and former Governor David Ige were in attendance. It was amazing how many people came to pay their respects.

On Friday, July 31, at sunset, the family and our closest friends gathered at Ewa Beach Park to scatter Roger's ashes. Yvette and I walked into the ocean to release the ashes. A large wave came and knocked us down. Everyone laughed and said Roger was playing a prank on us! I chose not to go further, so Yvette scattered some ashes, and Ryan took care of the rest. We took photos on the beach at sunset. It was beautiful.

I ordered thank-you notes from Shutterfly featuring Roger's photo on the cover. I ordered 150 for the Celebration of Life event and 600 for the memorial service. The sheer volume was overwhelming, so I hosted a thank-you card party. I bought all the stamps and called six friends who came over to help prepare the notes for mailing. I provided lunch, and we all had a wonderful time.

On the Sunday after Roger died, I began to cry a deep, guttural, and gut-wrenching cry. It felt like I couldn't stop. A close friend was there for me; she held me and let me cry my heart out. I had never cried like that in my life. I think my grief poured out that day, and afterward, I felt cleansed. I often cried during the first year, but not with that same deep, guttural pain. Each year, I cried less and less.

I arranged two one-year services: one on July 12, the anniversary of Roger's passing, and another the following month when my daughter and her family would be visiting Hawaii.

A funny thing happened on July 12, 2016. Fortunately, it was a Tuesday, so the golf gang was around. I went to pick up the food for Roger's one-year service but suddenly felt unwell, so I headed to the patio. When the weekly Tuesday golfers saw me, they said I looked pale, and they had me lying on the patio floor while they called 911. The ambulance picked me up, and I said, "Ironically, exactly one year ago, my husband was in an ambulance to Pali Momi when he died."

The paramedics gave me an EKG and IV fluids, which helped me feel better. At the Pali Momi ER, they took blood and conducted tests. While there were no positive results, they informed us that we had to wait two hours for another heart test. I declined, explaining that I needed to go home for a party!

Both services were held on my patio, attended by family, neighbors, and close friends. They were short, heartfelt gatherings, with guitar music and singing, and everyone shared one word to describe Roger. Both services were beautiful.

Lari's Path to Inspiration – A Facebook Post Two Years Later - part 2

Everyone goes through tough times in life. One of the hardest things is living life to the fullest and not allowing hardship to stop you from pursuing happiness. People experience breakups, lose their children, go through divorces, lose their parents, significant others, and homes, among other challenges. The ones I admire most are those who lift themselves up after the grieving period and choose to be happy.

Lari's Path to Inspiration – Lari Uplifts Kimberly - part 3

My Auntie Lari is the first person who comes to mind when I think of pure joy and happiness. After my Uncle Roger passed away, it would have been so easy for her to remain trapped in her grief. They did everything together: they traveled, laughed, and were best friends. Instead, my Auntie chose to be happy. She is always traveling, blogging about her adventures, trying new things, and still laughing and smiling. Whenever I have a bad day or feel stuck in my life, I visit her Facebook page to watch her videos. Her tenacity and infectious laugh brighten my day and help me realize there are bigger things to focus on than being stuck in a sad moment in time.

Dave Learns Numbers Connect Us to Heaven

Do you believe in love at first sight?

When I met Donna, I was a physical education teacher and a coach for baseball, basketball, and football. She taught math and coached cheerleading. One day, she brought us the roster to print, and within five minutes, I knew I wanted to marry her. After a few dates, I was sure it was love, and nine months later, we got married.

We were married for 35 years, with her battling brain cancer for 25 of those years—full of pain, suffering, and tears. My beautiful wife, who weighed 108 pounds, swelled to 178 pounds due to chemotherapy. Yet, she was "the best of all the rest." Before the cancer, we endured the loss of two children through miscarriage. After years of trying, Donna finally became pregnant and carried the baby to full term. Our beautiful son completed our family.

A problem, however, lurked in the shadows. Battling cancer for 25 years crushed our chances for sexual intimacy, or at least that's what I thought. It wasn't until just before she passed that Donna revealed she had endured childhood sexual abuse at the hands of her uncle, a priest.

So, between cancer and long-standing trauma, we couldn't enjoy the intimacy that most couples do. That was challenging for me, but I never wavered in my commitment to the marriage. I took an oath: "in sickness and in health." Besides, Donna was the greatest girl in the world.

Donna's passing was a difficult journey. My adult son and I constantly worried, "She's going to die, she's going to die," but she persisted. Such was her love for life...and for math! Donna tutored students in math every evening after a long day of teaching. She was the only teacher in New York who never had a student fail the state Regents exam.

For the first five years after her death, I could hardly speak, eat, or laugh. However, five months after she passed away, I experienced my first sign that she was watching over me. One scorching August day, my son and I were in the pool. There were no neighbors in sight and no golfers on the course. Yet, we found a golf ball in the pool with a single word on it: "Donna." I was deeply convinced that this was a breathtaking sign from her, filling me with a sense of wonder and connection.

During grief counseling, another sign appeared: hummingbirds. These delicate creatures often approached my window as if to say hello, and I was fascinated. Soon after, I discovered a small book called *Angel Numbers,* which had a profound impact on me and helped me through my grief. The book explains how each of the numbers 0 through 9 carries a distinct meaning related to God, heaven, angels, and connecting with departed loved ones. I started to see the number 1111 everywhere. Interestingly, the number 1 symbolizes a connection to heaven. I noticed 1111 on houses, license plates, digital clocks, and even menus. I would wake up at night and check my alarm clock, only to see it was 11:11 pm. Night after night. It felt like too much of a coincidence to ignore. No matter which numbers you see, angels are trying to communicate. You need to believe and stay open to their guidance.

Now, after 18 years, I can say my grief has softened, but I still miss my wife. I keep seeing the 1111 sequence, which means I am connected to heaven and, therefore, to Donna. I still talk to her. Whether you believe in angels and signs or not, they offer a positive way to live. I love knowing Donna remains a part of my life.

The Day After – Tonya Griffen

The air was impossibly thin the day you left this earth, a stark reminder of your absence hanging heavily in the atmosphere. Each attempt to breathe felt like inhaling through a broken straw—my throat constricted painfully, and a gnawing tightness gripped my stomach. Anger surged through me as I watched the world continue around me, blissfully unaware of the void your departure created. How can I navigate life without my best friend? My heart shattered that day, leaving me utterly devastated. Yet, despite the overwhelming sorrow, I forced myself to rise, knowing that surrendering to despair would cause my life to spiral into relentless anxiety.

I clung to the vibrant echoes of our laughter, each moment filled with joy until our bellies ached, and the countless meals we created together, each dish a testament to our bond—moments I hold close to my heart. I vividly remembered the surprise I planned for your birthday: a luxurious limousine whisking us away to Humphreys in San Diego, accompanied by four of our dearest friends, all gathered to enjoy the magic of Michael Franks' concert. Steffon, you were a musician by age three, your spirit intertwined with melodies and harmonies—music was our love language, a vital part of who we are.

In my darkest hours, your voice and smile became my lifelines, radiating warmth and comfort. Though you are gone, you remain forever etched in my heart, my angel, S.D. Harmon—the one who taught me the true meaning of unconditional love.

Janet Youngs-Norwood

Losing my late husband in a tragic accident was almost more than I could bear. I immediately found a local Grief Share class (offered through recreation centers, senior centers, churches, and even funeral homes) that provided me with the tools I needed to continue living, but in an entirely new way.

In that class, a friend and I coined the phrase "a new normal," acknowledging that life would never be the same. Our old lives were behind us, often accompanied by the loss of good friends. It was now up to each of us to make new friends, explore new horizons, and reach for new dreams.

That journey isn't easy and is often filled with moments of sadness and anxiety, but it is certainly one worth taking, especially when shared with others.

Celebrate Life with Bernie – Victoria Benoit

As I supported my husband Bernie, with whom I had shared ten years, through the final stages of his life, I reflected on my mortality. What would bring me more comfort if I were facing the end of my life's journey?

I would want to know if I made a difference in the lives of others.

My beloved Bernie was always interested, caring, and engaged with others. He would help anyone with anything. It occurred to me how great it would be for him to know his immense impact on others.

Why gather to express appreciation for someone only after they pass away? Why not do this while they are still alive? This inspired me to create a "Celebrate Life with Bernie" event—an opportunity for family and friends to share his impact on their lives. It would be a wonderful way to give him the recognition he deserved.

Over thirty-five people gathered to honor my beloved Bernie—standing room only. He sat in a comfortable recliner, thin and gaunt, without his prosthesis and with his oxygen tank by his side. He was so vulnerable and humble—that alone was incredibly inspirational.

I wanted everyone to share how Bernie had influenced their lives, but Bernie wanted no such thing. He wanted them to tell an uplifting story about their lives so everyone could be inspired. I began the celebration by welcoming everyone and reciting an inspirational poem.

Bernie then expressed his love for me:

"I want to share my little story. We all have certain songs and experiences that resonate deeply. It's the song "I Want to Know What Love Is" by Foreigner. When I first heard it in the 70s, the experience was so intense and powerful—I always wanted to understand what love truly means. I got married, had kids, and felt a profound love, even though that marriage didn't quite work out.

"It was very early in my relationship with Victoria that this song came back to me. I felt one of my life purposes was to experience love to the fullest, and I experienced it with Victoria, spiritually and physically—and it's extraordinary. So that means everything to me, and then, of course, we went on for many more years and had many more extraordinary experiences. It's been a wonderful life, yet I wasn't quite ready for where I am today. So, as they always say, live your life fully today—you don't know what may happen tomorrow."

Linda, the host, swiftly dismissed Bernie's idea of having everyone share an inspirational story from their own lives. She remarked, "Bernie, I know you don't want this to focus on you, but it's really about you." She expressed how much of an impact he had on her life as a friend and how helpful he had been, particularly when he fixed things around her home on many occasions.

One after another, people shared the difference Bernie made in their lives. He had so much energy that evening, unlike most evenings at home. It was beautiful to see. Bernie's youngest son and his girlfriend were there. It was heartwarming to watch them take in how Bernie had influenced the lives of so many people. My mom expressed her gratitude to Bernie for making me so happy, which made her happy and made Bernie really happy.

In the recesses of my heart, I was still whirling from Bernie's special words about me and our love. At that moment, it felt as if I was alone, yet people were everywhere. I listened intently and took to heart all the amazing things I heard. I was moved to tears several times, absorbing Bernie's positive impact on the people sharing.

Throughout the gathering, I sensed the guests knew this would be the last time they saw Bernie. It was palpable; tears were flowing. My heart was bursting with all the love in the room. My Celebrate Life with Bernie idea had worked. It was breathtaking to see how deeply moved he was by his positive impact on others. The next day, Bernie listened as I shared all the messages people wrote on the poster boards I decorated for the event. What a beautiful memory to engrave on his soul and carry with him on his journey home.

From Pieces to Peace: My Journey of Healing – Valorie Newman

Losing my husband and son has been the most challenging experience of my life. The pain of such immense loss is something that words alone cannot describe. Yet, through it all, I discovered a way to cope, heal, and eventually find peace: through singing and music.

I've been singing in church for as long as I can remember. Music has always provided an escape, allowing me to express my emotions and connect with something greater than myself. It has a melodic way of soothing my soul, acting as a muse that aids in healing from life's adversities.

I'll never forget Sunday, August 5, 2018, the day I suddenly lost my husband right in front of me. The struggle to save his life while panicking, performing CPR, and trying to communicate with the 911 operator still haunts me. It all happened so quickly. I knelt above his helpless body, watching his soul slip away.

When I realized I could do nothing to change things, bring him back, or even say, "I love you," a dark cloud of numbing grief consumed part of my being. I was overwhelmed by immense sorrow, a pain so deep that it erased my ability to eat, sleep, or even muster the strength to pray. God heard my cries and understood my moans when I could not speak. The days felt long, and the nights were even longer.

I couldn't imagine anything worse than the piercing, excruciating grief I had endured during this sorrowful time. Then, one week later, as I rose from the fetal position, I received the most unimaginable call ever... I lost my only son. This felt insurmountable, as if a part of my soul had been savagely ripped away.

I found myself seeking comfort in church and music. Singing became my sanctuary. The familiar hymns and songs were a balm for my aching heart. Through music, I could express my sorrow, my anger, and, ultimately, my hope. I've always heard people say that God does not put more on you than you can bear. I felt as if I had been hit by a Mack truck several times and left for dead. If this was God's way of reminding me that I am His child and of bringing me closer than ever to Him, He had my undivided attention! All I could do was pray day in and day out not to let depression, pain, and sorrow destroy my will to live, to stay strong for my 16-year-old daughter, who had lost both her father and brother.

It was a long and devastating journey, one that left me at the most mind-blowing crossroads of my life. It took months before I could listen to the radio again because every song brought back memories. I would abruptly change the station to avoid sentimental ballads. Sunday church service was also complicated, but it became my hope and inspiration in time. I returned to my music, and singing became a way to process my grief and release the pain that words could not express. Each note and melody were steps toward healing.

Music provided a way to connect with memories of my husband and son, honor their lives, and keep their spirits alive in my heart. Each song was a tribute to their love and the moments we shared. Singing helped me discover a sense of peace and a belief that they were still with me somehow.

As I performed, I felt a deep connection to them. It was as if they were listening and encouraging me to continue. Music became a bridge between the past and the present, linking my grief with my healing. I decided I wanted to make a record, and my debut album, *Spellbound,* was dedicated to them. Each song reflects my journey through loss and recovery. It stands as a testament to their memory and the love we shared. Through *Spellbound*, I channeled my emotions and created something beautiful from my pain, a tribute to their lasting presence in my life.

When I joined the cast of *The Color Purple: An American Musical*, I felt an immediate connection to the powerful story of resilience and redemption. Night after night, as I stepped into the role, I channeled my pain and healing into the character. The stage became a sacred space where I could express my deepest emotions and share them with an audience that unintentionally became part of my healing journey. In *Dreamgirls the Musical*, the cast's camaraderie and the raw emotion of the performances became my lifeline. Each song was a testament to the strength and beauty that can emerge from heartbreak. As I sang the soaring notes, I felt my spirit lift, rebuilding itself piece by piece.

Performing remains a vital part of my healing and renewal. As I stand backstage, the buzz of anticipation reverberates through the theater. The audience whispers and the lights dim, marking the start of another performance. I take a deep breath, focusing on the familiar comfort of the stage. The curtain rises, reminding me of the healing power of music and performance. As the first notes fill the theater, I step into the spotlight, ready to share my heart once again.

I thought I understood the meaning of the poem "Footprints in the Sand," but it wasn't until I went through my own painful journey that I truly grasped how I found the strength to get through. I realized that God carried me the entire way... from pieces to peace.

My Widow's Story – Ildryth

I knew him for over 36 years, and I wonder how much I ever knew him. He had secrets. Some secrets are just coming to light, a few years after his passing.

We met at a backyard party. He was sitting across the yard, listening intently to someone. He was nodding pleasantly. He was gorgeous. I was impressed. A friend told me he was married. But there he was, on a Saturday night, while his wife was... where? Later, I found out she was out gambling. She was addicted.

I saw him at parties over the next 18 years, and we always exchanged a few words. When Robert got divorced, we started dating. It seemed so easy because we had known each other for so long. I thought we were in love.

We had a casual wedding a few years later. I arranged everything because he was busy. I believed we were very happy during the first few years. Things were great as long as I handled most of the household chores, my own work, taking care of him, helping with his clients, and going to his fraternal organization events to be his eye candy. I was worn out. He increasingly pushed against my boundaries, like wanting me to stay up late when I was exhausted just to watch one more show. He kept bringing home more tools and devices that had no place to go. Once, he brought home a potted tree. Stuff started piling up in the house.

Robert had been an intelligence operative, and he took pride in quietly sneaking in and out of places. One terrifying night, he overstayed a meeting for hours and "snuck" into the house just before midnight. I could clearly hear his key in the front door and him moving through the house. Was that Robert, or a stranger? But he expected me to brush off the incident. No apology. Never mind my fear—or was he trying to make me afraid?

Robert started acting clearly mean and controlling. He was less and less the man I fell in love with. I realized that, while I married him to be married and to be life partners, he had married to be taken care of and to play mean games for fun.

Robert started sneaking to my office door when I had a client in, to listen to the conversation. Sometimes, he made sure to say, "That person really has problems, doesn't s/he?" He began closely watching my every move so that I couldn't call anyone for counseling or help. One day, I pretended I needed to get something from my car trunk to get a few minutes for an emergency call to a pastor friend.

Robert's health needed serious attention, but he refused to see any doctors, even though I kept the appointment schedule and drove him. His digestion was causing problems like enemas or cleanup, and sometimes he had bleeding. It was clear he was in a lot of pain. I said I simply couldn't do it all—I needed help—and he roared. By this time, I wasn't sure if he was imagining some things or consciously making them up. He let me know I was flirting too much with the men at his fraternal organization, pressing myself against them. That was his fantasy only. But he wanted to believe I was unfaithful, and he made up scenarios to support that belief.

Things took a turn when I was diagnosed with cancer—what a surprise—scheduled for surgery and a year of chemotherapy afterward. Days before my surgery, Robert was vomiting blood, and I called the paramedics. Robert went to the hospital for a few weeks. His son came from out of state and stayed with him a lot, sleeping in a friend's cottage. Since I was in pain and recovering from surgery, the silence and stillness at home felt heavenly. Robert passed in quiet comfort after five days in hospice. I was happy he no longer had any pain.

So then, what about me? My chemo year was painful and draining, yet also filled with peaceful quiet hours. Several years later, I am still working to restore my vitality. I have been increasingly learning to embrace my own life and to reshape my lifestyle.

Fortunately, many resources are available to those of us going through grief. I am mourning not only the loss of my husband, whom I loved deeply, but also the roughly 18 years I invested in that relationship. I have been attending hospice classes, receiving hospice counseling and regular therapy. I meditate, journal, and talk with close friends. The resources on narcissism have been particularly helpful for me. A church grief group helps me stay connected with other women who have lost long-term marriages. I am seeing friends more often and nurturing my own interests, including rebuilding my business. Living alone in a quiet house is truly wonderful.

Now I have the most peace I have experienced in over 20 years. I have been organizing his business files and mine, releasing computers, and swapping out furniture. I'm making my home more of my sanctuary and truly believe that my best recovery strategy is to understand the dynamics of my marriage and then live my best, happiest life. I am taking my revenge on any anger and frustration by redefining my life and living well. I believe the best is yet to come, and that's the path I choose to follow.

Love, Angels, and Butterflies – Jody Sharpe

When I lost my husband, Steve, after twenty-three years of marriage, I knew I had to go on, but it brought such heartache. Twenty years before his death, we had lost our precious daughter, Kate, in a car accident. At that time, I was beyond devastated. I thought I couldn't keep living without her. But I had our fifteen-year-old twins to care for, with Steve helping me through.

When Steve was diagnosed with cancer, a wonderful memory from months after Kate left the earth helped me through. A real miracle had impacted my life years before. As the months fell away after her passing, a dear teacher friend took me on a trip to Houston. The first day, we went shopping and met a man in an upscale store. My friend was purchasing something, and we said hello, telling him we were on a girls' trip. He told us he was there on business, and we said goodbye and went on our way.

To our surprise, the very next day, in a small gift shop in a town an hour away from Houston, he came up to us and said hello. It was surreal to see him again, and I can still picture him standing there tall and kind. He said, as if humorously, he'd see us at the airport. We laughed and, a little flustered, turned around to look at something, then turned back to say goodbye, but he was gone. It was like he had disappeared into thin air. We walked outside and looked up and down the street, but he was nowhere.

We both sat down at a little table outside the store and discussed the possibility he was an angel appearing to us as a human so I would know there really were angels and that Kate was safe in heaven. "See you at the airport," he had said, and those words spoke to me. My fear of flying had escalated since Kate's death. I sensed his unlikely presence would strengthen me. When we flew home, my fear had left me, and I began writing about grief. The thought of meeting an angel in human form inspired me to write novels about angels living as humans in a town where no one knows the secret. It was my therapy to write beautiful stories about angels, patterning them after my meeting the earthbound angel.

My first novel was published, and Steve was proud of my accomplishment. Then, as I wrote the second novel, Steve became ill with cancer. His three-year battle ensued, and I was right beside him. I knew, when Kate passed away suddenly, that there had been nothing I could do to bring her back. But Steve? I could find the care he needed, and he would beat the odds. Grit and determination took over. We went through it together as a team. I kept cheering him on. His bravery astonished me. He never showed self-pity, and I deeply admired him for that. We grew closer during the many hospital stays, doctor's appointments, and chemo and radiation treatments. We would win this battle together for sure, I thought. After all, I believed in angels and had met one. I prayed for Steve's healing. We became a stronger couple as we plowed along, but every turn brought more bad news for his survival. He trusted me and said I was his angel, but I didn't feel like one, just a wife trying to help her husband live. As the long road was ending, I spent extended days at the hospital, encouraging him with faith and hope in my heart.

One night, though, I didn't realize it would be our last quiet words of love for each other. The next day, he started to sleep all the time and stopped communicating. I felt I had failed. I had been so sure he would beat the odds. I prayed, believing in angels and miracles. But the reality was finally front and center. We all must die someday. It's a hard lesson to learn when you lose your child and then your husband. I thought Steve and I would go through our old age together, but it was not meant to be.

He slipped away in the early morning ten years ago. My son Mike and other family and friends were there. The reality was painful. I was suddenly a widow with no one to fight for. Weeks and months went by, and I kept going, as I had when Kate had passed away. Both times, I discovered a strength within me through the sorrow. I was resilient, a good friend told me. Our friends and family showered my children and me with kindness and support. Being able to count on them helped build my resilience.

An unexpected miracle happened after Steve passed away. I walked into the house, and I heard him call my name. I turned around, expecting to see his spirit, yet I had heard only his voice. I knew he was there to let me know he was watching over me. Steve was safe in God's hands like Kate was.

It had been three months, and I had my two pugs to care for and a life that kept me going forward. Yet, I wondered if I would ever write again. My creative gene seemed to have left with Steve's passing.

For my birthday, I flew to LA to spend it with my son Mike. My twins lived on opposite coasts, and I planned to see them as often as possible. I was learning to live without Steve, but would I ever be ready to write again? Writing was my soulful connection to God. However, that day, I learned that angels gave me a joyful answer.

Before Mike picked me up for my birthday dinner, he had dropped me off at a hotel near his apartment. I had stayed there before, but this time, the room had a window looking out directly onto the highway wall above. Surprisingly, the wall was breathtakingly covered in dense green vines with a myriad of blooming pink flowers. Delicately dipping in and out of the flowers were what I call tiny angels: precious butterflies. Looking out the window at the beauty of the scene was mesmerizing. I sat on the bed and stared for a long time; watching them filled my heart with gratefulness for being alive. I have always loved butterflies, so delicate as they light effortlessly on each flower and then fly on to the next. I drank in the miracle of earth's beautiful bounty.

Little did I know staying in that hotel room and visiting with Mike would change my grieving into a destiny of hope and writing. Creativity would beckon me back. You see, that evening at dinner, Mike gave me the most wonderful card. To my amazement, the front of the card was cut into the shape of a butterfly. Colorful glass jewels covered its wings, and it glistened in the shining candlelight on the restaurant table. A writer himself, Mike had written these sweet, thoughtful words: "Happy birthday, Mom. I know you will find your wings and fly again soon. Love, Mike"

I told Mike about the butterfly scene outside my window, and his butterfly card and loving words inspired me to write again. It seemed like a message from heaven above. I went home imagining the plot and characters of my third novel in the Mystic Bay series. It would be about an angel in town who sends butterflies to calm the saddened hearts of others. After publishing it, I wrote a children's book with the same theme. Over the last few years, I've written three more novels in the series and a memoir of my life teaching children with special needs. As time passes, I realize the serendipity of life has brought these moments, little miracles like the hotel's butterflies and my son's thoughtful birthday wishes. These moments are treasures we find through the sorrow of losing those we love. They help us keep going.

The memories of Steve are forever in my heart. It was an honor to take loving care of my husband. I am grateful for our time together and the years of love. Not long ago, I dreamed of him. He and a male companion rode bikes behind our house on the golf course pathway. Steve appeared young again; his hair was brown and tan, and he had on colorful shorts like he always wore. His back was to me, but I knew he was happy as he rode down the path on a sunny day. That's what heaven is like, I hope. Another world is waiting with our loved ones who have passed on before us.

I do believe angels are near, and sometimes we meet them unexpectedly. I believe also that little miracles find us. I know I was fortunate to meet the man I'm sure was an angel that long ago day. I think about him so often. Memories, finding joy in the little things, and loving the people here to love to keep me going. I have found my wings again. An ancient saying is framed on my wall to ponder each and every day:

"Just when the caterpillar thought the world was over, it became a butterfly."

Zhuang Zhou, Chinese philosopher, 4th Century BCE

Chapter 7 - Taking Care Of Business

When your spouse passes away, many administrative tasks must be handled. This process can feel overwhelming and draining, especially if you haven't been the one managing the bills, policies, and paperwork. Sorting everything out can be difficult, but it might also serve as a distraction from your grief. Although you may be tempted to stay in bed, all wrapped up under the covers, it's important to get up and face the realities and responsibilities that lie ahead.

The following list was compiled from websites, articles, and informational handouts provided by my financial advisor, Kyle Richardson, CFP® (Certified Financial Professional), Financial Advisor, and Fiduciary. With over 25 years of experience in the financial industry, Kyle specializes in creating customized retirement and legacy planning strategies, focusing on financial well-being. He has successfully passed the Series 7, Series 24, Series 63, Series 65, Series 66, and SIE exams, holds professional registrations with LPL Financial, and maintains Life, Health, and Variable Annuity licenses in Arizona and 30 other states.

Kyle takes pride in building long-term relationships with his clients. By establishing a foundation based on understanding each person's unique needs and goals, Kyle helps his clients visualize their future. He works with integrity, transparency, and persistence to support clients and their families in seeking financial independence.

In addition to numerous service awards recognizing his dedication to his clients and practice, Kyle's experience and expertise have also been acknowledged through multiple appearances on CNBC's *Squawk on the Street*, broadcasts on Bloomberg radio, and a featured article in *Forbes* magazine.

Financial Checklist for Surviving Spouses:

Losing a spouse triggers a flood of emotions that can make managing financial obligations feel nearly impossible. This checklist is designed to help those navigating this difficult time stay organized and make the next financial steps as straightforward as possible.

If possible, ask a family member or close friend for help. It can be very hard to stay focused during this emotional time. A helping hand can significantly ease the burden. If no loved one is available, consider hiring a financial advisor for assistance.

Gather all important documents in a central location where they are easy to access and work with. A large accordion folder can help keep things organized.

Documents to Gather:

Will/trust
Life insurance policy
Birth certificate
Marriage certificate
Death certificate (if you already have it)
Funeral arrangements or instructions
Social Security cards for both of you
Tax returns
Divorce agreements
Bank statements
Investment account statements
Stock certificates
Pension/retirement plan statements
Loan statements
Mortgages, leases

Deeds

Motor vehicle titles

Car insurance

Homeowner's insurance

Health insurance

Bills

Safe deposit box information (and key)

Storage locker contract

Business ownership or interest

Military service records

Computer records related to assets

Things to Do:

• Contact a funeral home to make arrangements for funeral preparations and payment. Ask the funeral director to help you get 12 certified copies of the death certificate or contact the County Clerk's office yourself to get them. There is usually a small charge for this.

• Contact your financial advisor (if you have one) so that the proper arrangements can be made for any survivor benefits, annuity payment plans, and payments to any designated beneficiaries to begin to be processed.

• Contact the Social Security Administration to notify them of the death. Be sure to let them know you are calling regarding spousal and survivor benefits.

• If applicable, contact your spouse's employer to inform them of the passing. Speak with the employer's human resources department directly so they can provide you with any paperwork that needs to be completed. Keep in mind that you may be due money because of your spouse's accrued vacation or sick time. Also, if you or your children were covered through your spouse's employer's medical insurance, ask about options for continuing the coverage, if you are interested in doing so.

• Contact an attorney to begin a review of your spouse's will, or if there is no will, to discuss how the probate process will work. The attorney will file the will with the probate court to have it approved.

• Make sure you have a plan in place for all your bills. Have all the bills put in your name. If you were not the one responsible for bills, research which were on automatic payment and which needed to be paid manually. One bank offers this guide: "Sign on to your account and access Bill Pay. You can add a payee manually, browse the list, or search by payee name. It's helpful to have recent copies of your bills available, so you can verify or enter each payee's name, address, and account number. Next, choose the payee you want to change. Select Edit or Delete Payee at the bottom of the payee's profile, make your changes, and save."

• Contact all credit unions or banks your spouse had accounts with to change the account holder information.

• If an active life insurance policy was in place, contact the provider. It can take several weeks to receive the funds, so try to get started as soon as possible.

• Contact providers of all other insurance policies – auto, homeowner's, credit card, accident, etc. – to let them know of the passing and to close or change the name on the policy.

• Check with all your spouse's former employers to see if they have any life insurance policies or other benefits for your spouse.

• Contact creditors to remove your spouse's name from any joint accounts and to close any accounts that were in your spouse's name only. Destroy any cards that were issued in your spouse's name. Let creditors know if the debts will be paid by your spouse's estate, or if not, how they will be handled. Your lawyer can help you with preparing this information.

• Send a letter to each of the three major credit bureaus (Equifax, Experian, and TransUnion) to get copies of your spouse's credit reports to ensure you are aware of all existing debts. In your letter, include:

1. Date of death.

2. Your name, address, relation to the deceased, and your signature.

3. The deceased's date of death, date of birth, place of birth, and addresses for the past five years.

4. Deceased's Social Security number.

5. A request that the deceased's credit report be mailed to you.

6. A request that the following notation be listed on the credit report: "Deceased – Do not issue credit."

7. Copy of marriage certificate and death certificate.

• Update the name listing on any deeds or titles, such as your home or your vehicles. Contact your state's Department of Motor Vehicles for the title changes to vehicles.

• If your spouse was in the military, contact the Veteran's Administration to learn what benefits you might be due.

• If your spouse belonged to a labor union, contact the union to see if they offer any assistance.

• If an illness or medical care preceded your spouse's passing, file a claim for the medical bills with your spouse's health insurance provider.

• Keep in mind that taxes for your spouse will still need to be filed for the year of death, and any taxes due will need to be paid. Since there could be estate taxes or other complicated issues to deal with, it is best to contact a tax professional to assist you.

• Cancel any clubs or memberships for your spouse, such as gyms or professional organizations.

• If your spouse had any business ownership or interests, contact the attorney who handled your spouse's business affairs to learn what steps need to be taken to handle any transitions. Also, contact any business clients your spouse may have been working with or for.

• If your benefits represent a large amount of money, consult with a financial advisor to put that money to work to achieve your goals.

• It is also good to reassess what your budget will look like going forward. Try to estimate how your expenses and income will change.

Bobbie's point of view

Information on what to do after your partner's death is easily accessible. I've included a few more ideas here.

I also gathered this information from my experiences with the first and second times my husband died. My first husband, who was well-connected, insisted on putting everything in my name: the house, the cars, the utilities, and the bank accounts. He understood that, in his world, anything in his name could be confiscated if he got into trouble. When he passed away, I didn't have to change a thing.

My second marriage ended in an amicable divorce. After dividing our shared credit card debt, we closed all our accounts to start anew.

The situation with my third and final husband was more challenging. When Clayton and I first met, we each owned our own homes. After we got married, we sold both properties and bought a new one together, with both of our names on the title.

For convenience, Clayton transferred the utilities from his home to our new home without adding my name. Since he insisted on paying the mortgage and utilities without my assistance, I didn't perceive any harm in excluding my name from the utilities. When he passed away, the utility companies requested a copy of his death certificate and conducted a credit check on me before allowing me to be added to their accounts.

It took several months to close specific accounts in Clayton's name because I was unaware of their existence. For instance, he was a Sunbeam Tiger Car Club member and received magazines quarterly. He also subscribed to other magazines that did not interest me and needed to be canceled.

Clayton and I established our personal credit cards before meeting and agreed to cover our purchases even after we married. Therefore, I didn't need to change mine; I just had to cancel his. In this way, we both enjoyed the independence of not needing to justify our spending. Many marriages could benefit from that!

Get Help

The lists I share in this chapter serve as a helpful guide to ease one of the most difficult times in your life. It can feel very overwhelming, especially when you're grieving, dealing with disturbed or sporadic sleep, and neglecting your own health and well-being. The sooner you can start taking care of yourself again, the better.

Now more than ever, it is crucial to seek and accept help from others. People often say, "If there's anything I can do for you, please don't hesitate to reach out." Aside from a few insincere individuals, most truly mean it. They want to help but feel awkward and unsure about how to assist you.

Consider your social network, if you are fortunate enough to have one, and determine who is suitable for each task. For example, don't ask a friend who only orders takeout to make a hearty casserole. Don't rely on someone who dislikes driving to run errands for you. Don't request that your neighbor, who can't stand dogs, walk Fido.

Now, your dog-phobic neighbor might be a great cook and would like to show her condolences by making and freezing a few dinners for you. Let her know! A friend who doesn't drive more than a mile might be a fantastic bookkeeper and would be perfect for helping with the administrative tasks mentioned here. Ask him or her!

Assume that the people who know and care about you genuinely want to help. Family and friends can offer a lot of support and insights, especially those who have experienced similar situations. This is not the time to pull back. It's also not the time to be stoic, stubborn, or try to prove you're a pillar of strength.

Staying focused during this emotional time can be tough, and having someone to support you can lighten the load. If no one is available to help, consider hiring a financial advisor. My financial advisor was priceless to me after Clayton passed away.

Stay Organized

Staying organized can be difficult. You should keep all important documents in a central location where you can access them easily. Use different colored folders to help you stay organized. You can also create a folder on your computer for documents you've already saved and for others you scan as you go along.

Accounts to Close/Change Name on the Policy

Closing accounts in your spouse's name or updating the account holder information can be a significant task after their passing. While it isn't difficult, it does take time. Make sure to request the necessary forms from your financial institutions.

You should review your list and check off each item as you finish it. Set realistic goals for yourself. Finishing it within a day or two might not be possible, no matter how efficient and capable you usually are. Give yourself several days or a week, but try not to let it take too long. Completing the task will give you a sense of achievement, which can help you stay calm and in control when your emotions and entire world feel overwhelming. These things should be on your list.

- Retirement accounts

- Bank-checking, savings, CDs, Venmo, Cash App, Google Pay, Zelle

- Credit Union

- Credit cards- department stores, big box stores, service stations, book-stores, airlines, etc.

- Mortgage or rental agreement

- Car loan

- Auto insurance

- Health insurance

- Homeowners/renters insurance

- Mortgage insurance

- Cell phone- Don't rush to cancel their cell phone. While your spouse's immediate family and friends will know of their demise, old friends and business contacts may not. Hold on to their phone for a few months and check messages weekly. You may find you need to return phone calls on your spouse's behalf.

That is exactly what happened to a friend of mine whose mother passed away suddenly. My friend was made a trustee of her mom's estate and was left with the complicated task of selling her condo in another state. She had no idea how to proceed or find a reliable realtor 3,000 miles away.

A couple of weeks later, her mom's cell phone rang.

"Hello, Sarah?" a man inquired excitedly.

"No, this is her daughter, Anna. Who is this?"

"This is Steve Eller, a good friend of Sarah's."

Anna swallowed hard, still struggling with saying the words aloud. "My mom passed away about a month ago."

"Oh, my God! What happened? I am so, so sorry. I loved your mom. I was her realtor when she bought her house and again when she sold it years later. I got her into her condo. We became good friends. I'm a Frank Sinatra impersonator, and she came to several of my shows. I loved seeing her smiling face in the audience and hearing her sing along. Nothing romantic between us. I'm a married guy and years younger than her, but we connected in a big way. I'm going to miss her terribly,'" he sniffled.

"Well, Steve, you just might be the answer to my prayers. I need to sell her condo. Can you help me with that?"

"Yes, yes, of course, I can sell the condo. I'll get you the best price possible. It's the least I can do for your beautiful mother."

And he did.

That conversation would not have happened if Anna jumped to disconnect her mom's cell phone. Sure, the condo would have sold, but with how much stress? Steve would have eventually found out about Sarah dying, but there was no closure.

Transfer ownership or cancel.

- Library card

- PayPal account in your spouse's name

- Landline telephone

- Cable television

- Internet

- Garbage & recycling

- Electric

- Gas

- Water

- Sewer

- Newspapers, including local, state/regional, and national

- Magazines

- Amazon

- Subscriptions and memberships (health clubs, country clubs, AAA, AARP, etc.)

- Contact the elections office to remove your spouse from the voter rolls.

- Wait to close email accounts and business or personal websites until you finish the estate process.

- Meet with your accountant/tax preparer. You need to file an income tax return for your spouse and an estate tax return during the year of your spouse's death. Keep track of bank statements and other important financial documents so you have everything you need when tax season rolls around.

Let's Talk Taxes

Taxes can be complicated, especially when you've lost a spouse. I wish I could give you advice that never changes, but I can't. Tax laws are always evolving and can differ by state. When my third husband died, I hired a tax professional, and I strongly suggest you do the same.

Without going into too much detail, how you file your tax returns depends on how long ago your spouse passed away. For example, you can typically use the Married Filing Jointly status in the year your spouse dies. Then, you can file your tax return for the following two years as a Qualifying Surviving Spouse unless you remarry during that tax year.

If you remarry in the same year your spouse dies, you cannot file a joint return with the deceased spouse. However, you can file as Married Filing Jointly with your new spouse. Additionally, you and your new spouse have the option to file separately.

The Qualifying Surviving Spouse status (formerly known as the Qualifying Widow or Widower tax status) can be claimed for the two tax years after your spouse's death, as long as *you meet the requirements*. However, even if you fulfill those requirements, you cannot use it for the year your spouse passed away. Sound confusing? I thought so, so I left it to a tax professional to figure out. Grieving is tough enough without having to navigate complicated tax language. Ugh!

Here's a heavy truth: being widowed no longer automatically means the surviving spouse inherits the deceased spouse's ownership of their marital property. That isn't always the case now. That marital property could go elsewhere, depending on whether the deceased spouse had a trust, a will, or based on the state they lived in. At the risk of sounding like a broken record, I'll say it again: seek advice from a tax expert, my friend.

Here's one last thought before we move on from the topic of taxes. Legally, the death of a spouse ends the marriage. This means widowed individuals are officially single and can remarry. If your spouse has passed away and you haven't remarried, you're considered *unmarried*. This might seem strange because you may still feel married and see yourself that way. After all, your wedding ring is still on your left fourth finger. But in the eyes of the law, your marriage ended with your spouse's death. There's nothing quite like the law to shock you into your new reality.

Is There More?

There is, but not much, so hang in there!

- Contact the Department of Motor Vehicles (DMV). Some states have a vital records department that notifies the DMV about a driver's death, automatically canceling their license. However, in states where this does not apply, the surviving spouse must terminate the license immediately to help prevent identity theft.

- To cancel a driver's license, you need to send a copy of the death certificate along with a letter to the state office that issues driver's licenses. You might have to schedule an in-person appointment, although many states allow you to cancel by mail. Check with the DMV to find out which forms and documents you must submit.

- Marriage certificate or divorce verification. If you lack proof of marriage or divorce, you can get a copy from the Vital Statistics Office in the state where the marriage or divorce took place.

- Divorce agreements. If your deceased spouse was previously divorced, a clause in the divorce settlement might require the estate to pay money or transfer other assets to a former spouse. Additionally, a former spouse may be legally entitled to part of the decedent's pension or IRA.

- Obtain military records. All honorably discharged veterans are eligible for funeral and burial benefits, including military honors at the funeral, burial in a military cemetery or a burial stipend, and a gravestone to mark the grave. If the veteran received a pension, the un-remarried surviving spouse and underage children may be eligible for survivor's benefits.

You will need a copy of the Veterans Form DD-214 (Report of Separation). Visit online to request a free copy of the form. You will also need a death certificate to access records of the deceased veteran.

- Contact college financial aid offices. If you have a child or children attending college, reach out to the school's financial aid office. They may qualify for additional financial aid and other benefits after losing a parent.

Selling Their Car

Owning a vehicle jointly with the deceased generally allows you to easily obtain full legal ownership. Once you contact the DMV and transfer the car title to your name, the vehicle becomes yours to sell.

Selling the vehicle should also be relatively straightforward if you are the deceased person's estate executor. The DMV might require specific paperwork and fees before the sale. You'll sign the title with your name and indicate your role as the executor for this sale. Then, transferring the title will be the buyer's responsibility.

Next Steps: Auto Insurance

Notify the insurance company about your spouse's death if you haven't already, and ask about the next steps. The surviving spouse or executor might inherit an auto policy that stays in effect after the driver passes away. In this situation, determine which driver is covered. Since the policyholder is changing, the car insurance premiums and discounts could also change.

Nevertheless, you still need to contact the insurance company to cancel the deceased car owner's auto policy. To prevent fraud, you might be asked to provide a copy of the death certificate and documents proving you are the estate executor.

Social Media

A few key points from my findings:

- Different platforms have different policies - some offer memorialization (like Facebook and Instagram) while others only allow deletion (like Snapchat and TikTok).

- Most platforms require proof of death, such as "a death certificate, obituary URL, or newspaper obituary scan," along with proof of your relationship to the deceased (Washington National).

- For some platforms, like TikTok, the only way to close an account may be if you already have access to its login credentials, which emphasizes the importance of password sharing between partners.

- If accounts remain active, there's an identity theft risk, as "scammers often troll newspaper obituaries" to collect information about deceased persons (Washington National).

- When handling linked accounts (like Pinterest connected to Google or Facebook), you should "deactivate their Pinterest before you delete the other social networks" (Dignity Funerals) to avoid complications.

The guide I've created also includes direct links to the relevant forms and contact information for each platform, presented in a clear, step-by-step format that would be helpful for someone dealing with grief while trying to manage these practical matters.

Closing or memorializing your partner's social media accounts is an important step in managing their digital legacy. This guide provides current instructions for the most common platforms.

Facebook

Options: Memorialize or delete the account

- Memorialize: The account will show "Remembering" before their name and remain visible to those who were already friends. No one can log in.

  - Go to: facebook.com/help/contact/234739086860192

  - You'll need to provide proof of death (obituary, death certificate)

- Delete: The account will be permanently removed.

  - Go to: facebook.com/help/contact/228813257197480

  - You'll need to provide the death certificate and proof that you're an immediate family member or executor

Instagram

Options: Memorialize or delete the account

- Memorialize: Similar to Facebook, "Remembering" appears before the name.

  - Go to: help.instagram.com/264154560391256

  - Provide proof of death (obituary link or death certificate)

- Delete: For permanent removal.

  - Use the same link above but select removal option

  - You'll need to provide death certificate and proof of your relationship

Twitter/X

Options: Delete account only (no memorialization option)

- Go to help.twitter.com and search for "deceased family member's account"

- Submit the form with your information

- Twitter will email requesting additional documentation including:

  ○ Your ID

  ○ Death certificate

  ○ Proof of relationship

YouTube/Google

YouTube accounts are managed through Google. To close:

- Go to: support.google.com/accounts/troubleshooter/6357590

- Complete the form

- Upload scans of the death certificate and your ID

Pinterest

- Email: care@pinterest.com

- Include:

  ○ Your loved one's Pinterest username

  ○ Your relationship to them

  ○ Proof of death (certificate or obituary)

  ○ Proof of your relationship (if not evident in obituary)

TikTok

TikTok has limited options for deceased accounts:

- Email: privacy@tiktok.com

- Include:

  - Your loved one's username

  - Proof of death

  - Proof that you're an immediate family member

LinkedIn
- Submit removal request: linkedin.com/help/linkedin/ask/ts-rdmlp

- Provide:

  - Their name and profile URL

  - Your relationship to them

  - Their email address and date of passing

  - Link to obituary

  - Their most recent employer

Snapchat
Snapchat will only delete accounts (no memorialization):
- Contact through support center

- Provide death certificate

- No access will be granted to account content

Important Tips
- Guard against identity theft:_Close accounts promptly as scammers may target profiles of the deceased.

- Preserve memories: Download photos and videos before deleting accounts.

- Plan ahead: Consider discussing with your partner what they'd prefer done with their accounts.

- Use a tracking system: Create a spreadsheet to monitor which accounts you've addressed.

- Be patient: This process takes time and can be emotionally taxing.

Remember, managing these accounts is not just about digital housekeeping—it's part of your grieving journey. Take breaks when needed and don't hesitate to ask for help from friends or family members.

What's in a Name?

Many believe that a woman must keep her husband's name after a divorce or his death. Not at all! This is a personal choice, not a requirement. You have the right to define your own identity and celebrate your individuality.

A woman I know kept her ex-husband's last name, Cook, for years after their divorce because it was easy to spell and never mispronounced. She didn't want to go back to her maiden name, Giglio. (Are those hard Gs, soft Gs, or one of each?)

Years later, this woman remarried, and her new husband soon passed away. She chose to keep his last name, Lipshitz, despite it being the subject of many jokes. When asked why she kept it, she said, "I was too lazy to change all my documents." When she died, her children decided not to engrave Lipshitz, Cook, or Giglio on her headstone. Instead, they inscribed only her first name, *Sharla*, as if she were a celebrity like Cher or Madonna. Gotta love that!

Bobbie's Ending Remarks

Discovering unknown accounts and subscriptions is one of the most overwhelming parts of losing a spouse. You're not alone in feeling surprised by what you find—this happens to nearly everyone.

Start with the mail. Collect every piece of mail for at least three to four months, even junk mail. You'll be amazed at what shows up: gym memberships, magazine subscriptions, streaming services, insurance policies, and credit cards you never knew existed. Set up a simple box or folder to catch everything.

Get multiple death certificates. Order at least 10-15 certified copies from the funeral home or vital records office. Companies won't accept photocopies, and you'll use more than you expect. Banks, insurance companies, investment firms, and even phone companies will each want their own copy.

Expect credit checks. When transferring utilities, cell phones, or credit accounts to your name, companies often require new applications and credit checks, even if you were married for decades. This isn't personal—it's standard procedure. Don't let it discourage you.

Create your tracking system early. Use whatever works for you—a notebook, smartphone notes, or a simple spreadsheet. Track the company name, account number, whether you've contacted them, what they required, and the outcome. This saves you from having to call the same company twice and helps you track your progress.

Watch for the sneaky ones. Annual memberships, professional associations, software licenses, and subscription boxes often bill just once a year. Some may not appear until months later. Warehouse clubs, AAA memberships, and alumni associations are commonly forgotten.

Prioritize what matters most. Handle essential services first—utilities, mortgage, car payments, and health insurance. Magazine subscriptions and streaming services can wait. Focus on what keeps your daily life running smoothly.

Ask for help when you need it. Many companies have dedicated bereavement departments with staff trained to be patient and understanding. Don't hesitate to mention that you're a surviving spouse—most representatives will be more helpful and may waive fees or expedite the process.

Be patient with yourself. Some days you'll tackle five accounts; other days you won't have the energy for one. Both are okay. This process typically takes six months to a year to complete fully, which is normal.

Remember: every account you handle is progress, not just paperwork. You're building your new life, one step at a time, and you're stronger than you know.

Chapter 8 - To Date Or Not To Date

My life has been filled with many experiences, some good and others not so good. I've learned to accept both the positive and negative, and I realize that I was lucky when it comes to relationships. My late husband, Clayton, had a servant's heart for me. He did little things that made me feel special and appreciated, like opening my car door and helping me with my chair at restaurants. Despite his old-fashioned and gallant gestures, we always respected each other's decisions, even when we disagreed.

Thinking about dating after losing a spouse or partner can be tough. In today's world, where traditional roles are often unclear, navigating the dating scene can be confusing. Open communication and mutual respect are essential for building any relationship. These qualities, along with humor, are very important. Never underestimate the power of laughter when facing life's challenges. Your "bad" dating stories can become funny ones if you approach life with a relaxed attitude and a good sense of humor.

Regarding moving on with someone else, I feel very comfortable with my life. I have gotten used to living alone without feeling lonely. My grandkids, writing, involvement in show business, and social media keep me busy. When you've experienced the best, there's a deep sense of satisfaction that, for me, is enough.

So, I decided to interview people who have more dating experience after experiencing a loss. It's refreshing to hear their honest stories. Entering the dating scene after losing a spouse can be intimidating and unsettling. Before dipping your toes in the water, it's important to be clear about who you are and what you value. For those who spent years caring for a spouse battling cancer or other degenerative diseases, you deserve all the happiness in the world. God bless you!

However, there can be significant judgment about your choices regarding whom to engage with after your spouse has died. Sadly, people often feel compelled to interfere in others' lives. The grieving process varies from person to person. No one can decide who, what, or when dating is appropriate for you. Some grieve for months or even years, while others move on faster, so ignore attempts to conform to someone else's timeline or expectations.

How do you know you're ready to date? By the time you start thinking about it, you've likely moved past the intense stages of grief and are on the other side. You're reconnecting with life and finding joy in simple, meaningful moments. You're taking good care of yourself physically, emotionally, and spiritually. You don't *need* someone as much as you want to share meaningful experiences with them.

It's okay to date if you're lonely or seeking companionship, but you should understand it won't heal the pain of losing a spouse. Healing takes time and effort to stay positive and find activities that help others while you're healing. It's unfair to expect dating to fix your deep loss. Dating provides chances to make new friends and experience special moments, including building stronger relationships.

Experts agree that discussing your past marriage or partner with someone you're dating is acceptable. They will naturally be curious, so feel free to share. Avoid dwelling on the past or going into detail about how wonderful your former partner was. Not only is that tedious, but who can compete with a ghost? The person you're dating needs to see that you're ready to move on.

Some people mistakenly treat their dating partner like a life coach or therapist. They share feelings of missing their spouse, feeling sad, and guilt over everything said and unsaid. If you're in this situation, it's best to seek help from a professional. It might also be helpful to take a break from dating for a while, and that's completely okay. Remember, this is a healing journey and process.

You don't need to explain or defend your decision to date again. Ideally, your family and friends will respect your choice and be happy for you. If they mistreat or disrespect the person you're dating or keep mentioning your deceased spouse in front of them, you should address that calmly, lovingly, and assertively. If you're unable or unwilling to do so, it might mean you're not ready to get back into the dating scene.

Losing your life partner means losing intimacy and physical connection. The thought of "getting physical" with someone new can excite one person, while another might feel nervous or intimidated. Take it slow. Get to know each other well. Make sure there's a foundation of mutual trust and respect before sharing your body and soul.

Dating in Today's World

If you've been out of the dating scene for a while, you might come across new terms like ghosting, zombie-ing, breadcrumbing, and benching. These words describe behaviors you should recognize when dating. Whether online or in person, being a knowledgeable dater is essential!

Ghosting happens when someone disappears, meaning they go off the grid, after you've been seeing or communicating with them regularly. Please avoid doing this to others, and be wary of anyone who does it to you. Zombie-ing is when someone ghosts and then comes back from "the dead." It sounds crazy, right? They ignore you, and weeks or months later, they reappear out of nowhere, wanting to start fresh. That's a red flag.

Breadcrumbing occurs when someone is non-committal but engages in actions that make you believe you have a chance at exclusivity, even though you don't. Essentially, they only give you breadcrumbs. You deserve more than that, so why settle for crumbs when you should have the whole loaf? Stay away from them.

Benching means you're someone's backup while they explore other options. They're out on the field, but you've been benched like a junior varsity player. You shouldn't be benched. You're a star player, so switch teams and do it fast!

All this new jargon and strange dating behaviors can make dating feel overwhelming. Please don't be discouraged or disheartened. Knowledge is power. Stay informed and smart, but remember that most people are honest, respectful individuals seeking a meaningful connection. I'm confident you will eventually figure out who deserves your time, energy, attention, and affection.

Now, let's jump into the dating stories!

He Danced His Way into My Heart

When my second husband, Arnie, passed away, our son, Brian, was nearing the end of high school. I had to accompany him on school visits and help him prepare for college, putting aside my grief. There are priorities in life, and life is for the living. Helping him get ready for college helped distract me from my sadness.

When Brian went off to school and I was nearing 60, I decided to take ballroom dancing lessons. Arnie and I were introduced to it on a cruise. We enjoyed it and talked about continuing once we became empty nesters.

I took some private dance lessons to learn quickly and enjoyed them immensely. I then started group lessons, where I met Jack, which, of course, felt like fate. His wife had passed away, and he found joy in the lessons, so we had that in common. Jack and I became friends and dance partners. Meanwhile, I was exploring various online dating sites and going on dates here and there. I was so passionate about dancing that it became a deal breaker if I met a man who showed no interest in it, or at least no desire to learn.

A year went by, and Jack asked me out. We were already good friends who knew a lot about each other's lives and families. Now, it was time to take our relationship to the next level. Before long, we became a strong couple.

In addition to dancing, we found joy in concerts, theater, traveling, and spending time with family. We took cruises and visited Las Vegas, California, and Europe. During our trip to New York City, we stayed in Times Square and attended an early matinee followed by another evening show. For 12 wonderful years, we were incredibly happy. Jack's family cherished his happiness, so they loved me and always included me in family gatherings.

Then Jack fell ill. The doctors discovered a tumor near his pituitary gland in the brain, wrapped around the optic nerve. They surgically removed most of the tumor through his nostrils, avoiding incisions and scars on Jack's handsome face. Amazing. They performed a series of targeted radiation treatments with a CyberKnife to eliminate the remaining tumor cells and preserve his vision. Everything went smoothly; Jack appeared fine, and life was good. Two and a half years later, Jack started to lose his eyesight and eventually went blind.

I became Jack's only caretaker after his adult daughter died, and all his relatives were aging. Being blind was emotionally tough for Jack because he was active, energetic, and athletic. My presence in his life made things easier for him. He trusted me with his financial affairs and appointed me as his medical proxy, giving me the duty to handle everything. I went with him to all his appointments and took him to the gym to use the treadmill, helping him keep his circulation and stay sharp.

Eventually, Jack needed 24/7 care. I found a facility, moved him in, and visited him every day. He was such a kind man that it was hard to leave him. The facility's staff said I was definitely going to heaven.

Jack died six years ago. I discovered that once you're on a dating site, you can still receive and reply to messages. I dated a little, but most men in their 70s look for women who are 10, 15, or even 20 years younger. I may be fit and attractive, but my age is a barrier for them. Age can also be a barrier for me. How many years of good health can I expect from a man approaching 80? Many men in that age group are facing health issues. I don't want to be a caretaker again, so I've stopped dating.

I thought about returning to dancing, but since COVID-19, I no longer enjoy an activity where faces are almost touching. I miss it, but the fear of catching something lessens my enthusiasm.

I may be alone, but I am never lonely. I belong to a weekly choral group and the choir at my synagogue. I am also part of an art group that explores media ranging from makeup artistry to meditative doodling and neurography—I even taught a class on it! Additionally, I take courses at a local college and have a wonderful network of female friends with whom I can discuss everything from intimate life details to politics and current events.

Lastly, I have a daughter and two grandsons whom I visit in New York. I bring art projects for the boys and me to work on together. They know and love me and will remember me when I'm gone. I cherish my role as a grandmother. My son lives in Florida, not far from me, and we occasionally get together for lunch or to shop at Costco. He is always there if I need anything.

It's funny; I was married twice and had a child with each of my two husbands, but Jack was the love of my life. I would never have met him if it weren't for my passion for dancing and my determination to move forward in life.

No One-Night Stands

I started dating about a year after my husband passed away. At first, it felt strange. I listened to these men talk about what they were looking for in a woman. Most of them saw relationships as one-sided; it was all about them, their needs, wants, and desires. They seemed eager to pick up where they left off with their deceased wives. Furthermore, sex was a major priority! I was shocked to discover that sex was expected after dinner on the first date. I'm not a prude; I genuinely believe that intimacy in the bedroom should involve more than just a meal.

Ready to Take a Chance Again

I didn't start dating until five years after my wife, Donna, passed away from brain cancer. When I finally began dating, I learned a lot. After going on several dates with different women, I discovered what women generally want. In short, I found that women look for money, security, and an understanding of what you can offer them. My main goal in dating was to see if and how we could bring out the best in each other. Unfortunately, most women and I felt like we were worlds apart.

One lady wanted me to pay off her three mortgages. I was glad I had just paid off my own! Another woman said, "If you buy me this bracelet, I'll give you sex." We didn't even know each other, so that was a no. A third woman said, "If this goes well, I'm heading to Victoria's Secret for new underwear." It ended up being our first and last date. A month later, I heard she got married. Another woman revealed she had herpes and asked, "Is that going to matter to you?" Yep, that was a deal breaker. I guess these experiences put a damper on dating for me.

Then Bonnie came along.

Almost three years ago, Bonnie and I met at the gym I go to every day. Physical fitness has always been important to me. We got along well, and after a few dates, she invited me to her timeshare in Mexico. During the drive down, I wondered if it would be a one-bedroom or two. It was a two-bedroom. I felt relieved. It had been a long time since I used that equipment.

It wasn't long before I met Bonnie's social circle. Her family loves me now, her friends adore me, and most importantly, her dog is fond of me. We hold hands, dance together, go to shows, and have taken a few vacations, but sex is off the table for her.

I managed to deal with the almost complete lack of intimacy with my wife, Donna, so I might be the only man who can succeed in this situation. We are planning our next vacation in Mexico, and I can only hope for the best.

I'm thankful to have a wonderful woman in my life and to be in love. Honestly, after two heart attacks, I'm grateful just to be alive. The biggest lesson I've learned is that, despite life's struggles, love wins. Never give up on love.

Keepin' It Old School

I'm 52 years old and ready to continue my life journey. It's been years since I lost my soulmate, and I don't expect to replace him. However, I love to travel and enjoy good food. I wouldn't say I love doing these things alone. I've joined a few singles groups to meet like-minded people who love to laugh and are open to adventure. If intimacy feels right, I'm open to it if we keep it traditional!

Blurred Lines

Navigating the dating scene in my 60s has been quite a challenge. In my younger days, I often followed a more traditional approach. I took pride in opening car doors and helping my date get settled at her restaurant chair. Those simple acts felt like small but meaningful ways to show my respect and admiration.

The world has changed a lot. Many women I meet are strong, independent, and assertive. They eagerly take charge and make their own decisions. I truly admire women who believe in themselves and value their independence. Sometimes, I wonder where I fit into this unfamiliar world. I see confidence and self-sufficiency radiating from those around me, which makes me feel like an outsider. I'm willing to wait for the right person who appreciates my values, not just as a relic of the past.

The Future Looks Bright

I was married to the same man for 46 years. For most of our marriage, we lived in a modest home in a quiet neighborhood. We raised four loving boys who continue to bring joy to my life. I have nine grandchildren and one great-grandchild. Family and close friends have always surrounded me.

My husband's close friend, Bill, who lives next door, always helped me when I needed it. Bill is what I call a true friend. He's a quiet man and a good listener, someone I can talk to without judgment. It only seemed natural to continue our friendship after my husband passed away. I'm unsure what the future holds for us, but I feel blessed to have Bill in my life.

Around The Water Cooler

I started dating a coworker four months after losing my wife in a fatal car accident. I wasn't ready for all the drama at work. Some claimed we were having an affair before my wife died, while others argued it was too soon for me to date and that I needed more time to grieve. Rumors said she was taking advantage of me in my vulnerable state. I wasn't looking to replace my wife; I just wanted companionship, someone to help me stay in the present. Moving on isn't always easy.

Open-minded in Cleveland

After losing my spouse, I never expected to be in another relationship. Still, I found comfort with a widower from my grief support group. Although we have different personalities, we became close friends and eventually started dating. It's been nearly a year, and I am amazed at how well we've adjusted. I'm thankful for keeping an open mind about dating someone different from my late husband.

Online Dating a Hit

After my husband passed away, I decided to start dating again after five months. This wasn't a sudden choice but a desire to live my life in a way that would honor him. My husband had fought diabetes for three years, and during that time, I embraced my role as his caregiver. He always wanted me to be happy, and I realized that occasional dating would be a positive step forward. I wasn't looking for anything serious, just a movie or dinner out here and there. I felt ready for this because of the challenges my husband and I faced during those three years.

I joined a dating site focused on people 50 and over. I hesitated to meet men through this platform, but after a few dates, I found it interesting and fun. I'm not trying to replace my husband, but I enjoy going out and meeting new people.

Too Good to Be True

After my wife passed away, I missed our date nights. So, I decided to create a profile on a dating app. I wasn't looking for anything serious, just someone to spend time with now and then. However, as I started getting responses, I became more interested in companionship. Out of all the women who responded, one caught my eye. Let's call her Bella.

Bella's sports knowledge impressed me, and she enjoyed dancing. We connected instantly. Before I realized it, my calendar was filled with baseball games, live theater, performances, elegant dinners, and dancing. It felt like I had found my soulmate without the need for marriage vows.

After six months filled with laughter and intimate evenings, Bella came to me with a dilemma. She was struggling to keep up with her mortgage payments. I offered to help but made it clear it would need to be in the form of a loan. I never imagined it could be a setup. That kind of thing only happens to widows who fall prey to con artists. However, I began to worry when Bella started asking for more money for car repairs and a medical procedure her insurance wouldn't cover. I hired a private detective to do some checking... just like in the movies. It was a good decision I did. Turns out she had scammed several other guys with her sob stories.

I learned my lesson the hard way: if something sounds too good to be true, it probably is. Although I still enjoy using a dating app to meet other women, now I know what to watch out for. I will no longer lend money!

Cruise Line Companions

After 22 wonderful years of marriage, my beloved wife lost her battle with lung cancer. As her primary caregiver, I dedicated myself completely to her, whether comforting her through painful nights or sharing quiet laughter over treasured memories. Although she is no longer with us, her vibrant spirit and the countless memories we shared will remain forever in my heart.

Six months ago, I went on a singles cruise to escape life as a widower and find new adventures. There, I met an exciting woman; our connection was instant and electric. Since we live in different states, we've had several meaningful phone conversations, shared dreams, and enjoyed planning another cruise together. Currently, we're settling into our roles as cruise line companions. I eagerly look forward to where this next chapter in my life will take me.

HUGE Mistake Averted

I was married for 25 years to the father of my three children. Our marriage ended in an amicable divorce, and we remained friends until he died at 87. Several years after our divorce, I married a man who passed away just after our fifth wedding anniversary. A few years later, I decided to start dating again. My dating stories could fill a book, but one story stands out in my mind.

I met a man, let's call him Steve, on a dating site, and after a pleasant phone conversation, we decided to meet locally for coffee. Not a bad-looking guy, tall and soft-spoken. After some friendly banter, he said, "Stacy, I have a problem. I get a lot of first dates with nice women, but none of them want to have sex with me because I have a huge penis, and it scares them off." Talk about being taken aback! What a bizarre thing to say on a meet-and-greet coffee date.

You have got to be kidding. Is this some kind of joke?

Steve looked at me sheepishly and said, "I wish it were. I saw on your dating profile that you are Jewish. I have never dated a Jewish woman before. Maybe Jewish gals are more...ahem...accommodating."

I replied, "Steve, I don't believe a word you are saying. If this penis of yours is as big as you claim, I have got to see it."

With that, we left the diner and got in my car; he unzipped his trousers and pulled out his member. Oh, my God! It was the largest male appendage I had ever seen, even in its flaccid state. Saying it was intimidating is an understatement. It was otherworldly, and it marked the end of the line for Steve and me. I felt sorry for the man, and as much as I can appreciate some length and girth, I wanted nothing to do with that mammoth phallus!

Although it took me a few months to return to online dating, I'm glad I did. I met a wonderful man, and we went out for six years. After we parted ways, I dated another man for nearly eight years. By the time that relationship fizzled out, I was approaching 80. Since guys my age are looking for younger women, and I'm not interested in an older man, I decided my dating days were over. I still remember what I saw in my car outside the diner. As they say, "Once you see something, you can't unsee it." Now, it just makes me chuckle.

Being Single Sucks

One sunny afternoon, my retired neighbor Joe, a well-meaning but somewhat shy man, approached me and asked how he could meet a lovely lady to spend quality time with. I knew that Joe had been struggling with loneliness since his wife passed away two years ago. He shared his weariness of eating out alone, attending concerts without a partner, and sitting at events feeling like an outsider among couples. He kept saying, "Being single sucks." I could tell he longed for more than just a social companion; he wanted someone to share the rest of his life with.

Joe hadn't been part of the bar scene since he quit drinking years ago, so I suggested places that offered a variety of non-alcoholic options, including creative mocktails and artisanal sodas. This way, he could enjoy gatherings while feeling comfortable and included among friends. He might also enjoy local dance studios, where dancers of all levels can connect through music. Another idea was to volunteer at places he found fulfilling, like botanical gardens, coaching, helping with community projects, or serving as a docent at various historical sites.

A month later, Joe sent me a bouquet of roses along with a thank-you card that read, "Being single doesn't suck anymore!"

Right Under My Nose – Victoria Benoit

My husband Bernie and I shared a special love. In fact, our love kept growing until the moment he passed away. He encouraged me to love again and to find something even greater than what we had. I couldn't believe that such a love existed or that I would be ready for it anytime soon.

There was a lot to do after Bernie released his soul from his physical body on 11-27-17. I wasn't ready to sell the house, but I wanted to turn the front bedroom into a home office. Bernie's best friend, Robert, was enthusiastic about the project and stayed with me during the three-month renovation for convenience and time. We had been friends for ten years and enjoyed each other's company, but we both still missed Bernie.

While working on the room, Robert repaired the ceiling and roof, installed a new carpet, added crown molding and new baseboards, installed a new window and ceiling light, and built contractor-quality shelves to store my office supplies. What a guy!

Believe it or not, I began receiving messages from Bernie. His voice echoed in my mind as I journaled. His words comforted, healed, and surprised me. One day, he said, *"You don't need my permission for anything; however, I want you to know it's okay to make love with someone else. I'm working on sending you someone magnificent."* It was exhilarating to still feel his love for me. *I love you too, Bernie!*

Just three months after my beloved's passing, I was fully focused on moving forward. I felt moments of sadness, frustration, and longing for Bernie, but I was prepared to re-engage with life. My friend Donna visited for a few days, and we had an amazing time. I felt completely supported. After she left, I was surprised when a short-lived romance appeared.

While Robert was working in my office, a connection grew between us. We started cuddling and kissing now and then—though it felt a bit too soon, and OMG, with Bernie's best friend? It seemed like I was betraying Bernie, but then I remembered he told me not to wait for love. Robert, however, wasn't ready for a relationship. He was totally dedicated to his spiritual journey. I understood and respected his focus on personal growth and expansion. Then he left, and we didn't talk for the next two years.

A few months later, I decided it was time to get back into the dating scene. Following a friend's suggestion, I bought the book *Getting Naked Again* by Judith Sills, PhD, and spent the weekend reading it.

I set out to find what kind of man would be right for me despite the author's warning that there might be some heartbreaks along the way. She also assured me that a great partner would eventually come along.

Dancing is one of my main social activities, and it's where I met most of the men I dated, including Vince. Vince and I went out for drinks and enjoyed getting to know each other better. After dating twice a week, we spent a fun weekend in Rocky Point, Mexico. On the drive home, we argued about the timeshare presentation we attended. He didn't want to discuss it, so we drove back to Phoenix in silence. RED FLAG #1!

The week after our trip to Mexico, I casually mentioned to Vince that I wanted the huge lantana bush in my front yard trimmed. He thought I should remove it altogether, but I was determined to keep it. He generously hired a landscaper to do the work. When I came home, my beloved lantana was gone. I was stunned. When I called Vince to let him know how upset I was that he had disregarded my wishes, he was clueless about why I was so upset. He offered to buy a replacement plant, but that was not the point. The point was that he deliberately did what I clearly asked him not to. RED FLAG #2!!

I started to notice how often Vince questioned me about where I went, what I was doing, and who I was with—it was unsettling. I'm a free spirit who loves being social with people while doing things I enjoy whenever I want. It became clear that Vince expected me to be someone other than who I am. RED FLAG #3!!!

After dating Vince for a couple of months, I realized I didn't want someone who controlled me—a valuable lesson to learn. What a wild start to my search for a new romantic partner. I avoided the dating scene for the next few months.

During the first week of December, I attended a meditation retreat in Cancun, Mexico, and met Allen, a Canadian. The first few evenings, he joined a friend and me for dinner, then we dined alone. He was divorced, and his conversation indicated he was ready to move on. I wondered how a long-distance relationship would work.

Allen visited me twice in January, and we had a great time! We shared a lot in common, and he wanted to strengthen our connection. I truly thought we'd stay in touch. Then, two weeks after his last visit, he ghosted me! No emails, no calls, nothing at all. Ouch! I had opened my heart to him, so this really hurt. I forgot to check my own rule about not dating anyone unless they had been out of a major relationship for at least a year and had no rebounds.

Bernie sent me a message encouraging me to love again and said he would help me find a great guy. Well, it hasn't been working out so far. *Bernie, you're sending me all the wrong guys.*

By April, I was ready to find new love. The dance studios had closed during the pandemic. I tried online dating instead, but the men I matched with were disappointing.

Allen from Canada reached out to me unexpectedly. He apologized sincerely for going off the radar and assured me he wouldn't do it again. He asked if we could start getting to know each other better, and I agreed. We FaceTimed for a couple of months, then...ghosted again!

Despite everything, I stayed open to love and didn't give up. I knew I was destined for another great love—someday.

I started thinking about Robert, so I called to check on him. We had a great conversation, and he offered to come over to look at some paint cans stored in the laundry room. I accepted his offer, and after examining the paint, he fixed the toilet in the apartment bathroom. After two years, it was nice to catch up while working on several projects together.

In the meantime, I actively deepened my relationship with Jesus. Being a new Christian happily took up much of my time. Since I hoped to develop a relationship with a man who also thirsted to know Jesus, I updated my spiritual affiliation on my online dating profile. I thought I would find more compatible matches. Wrong! Where were all the good men?

I thank God for Robert. After I moved in July 2021, he helped me with many projects in my new townhouse. He stayed in my second bedroom for a few weeks, and we resumed our deep, meaningful conversations.

Our friendship deepened and grew. At first, I was hesitant to pursue anything beyond companionship because I wanted to respect Robert's wish to continue his spiritual journey. He confessed that after Bernie died, he was afraid to enter an intimate relationship with me. Robert shared that he'd been divorced for fifteen years and had never considered another relationship.

To my surprise, one evening, while Robert and I were watching a movie, he leaned over and kissed me. He told me he had finished his spiritual pursuits and was open to whatever life would bring next.

After Robert returned home, we got together every week. I'd make dinner, and we'd watch a movie, cuddle, and kiss. Although there was no commitment to exclusivity, we enjoyed each other's company. It was too soon to know where we were headed, but I knew I was happy, and our friendship felt comfortable and intimate.

It's funny, but before our budding romance started, I hoped to find a Christian man who could dance, yet Robert was neither.

In mid-September, while dancing at the Arizona American Italian Club, I met Karl, a kind Christian man. We started seeing each other once a week, but unfortunately, Karl was not available between dates. The day after I attended my first fellowship service with Karl, Robert and I headed off to Breezy Pines for a week-long, off-the-grid escape from working on projects around my house.

After our trip to Breezy Pines and a few more dates with Karl, I realized I had a deep love and an undeniable friendship with Robert. I stopped seeing Karl, who later became my Bible mentor.

Because Robert and I were so compatible, my desire to date a Christian man who danced faded. To his credit, Robert tried dancing lessons, but we soon discovered he had two left feet. Oh, well, Bernie couldn't dance either.

Robert and I enjoyed a wonderful autumn filled with talking, cooking, watching movies, hiking, and decorating my townhouse. We also had a great time kayaking. I felt like a princess being floated around by my loyal knight.

As Robert and I grew closer, I felt uncomfortable with everything he did for me, like washing the dishes, scrubbing the floor, and taking care of my car. He told me to get used to it, and eventually, I accepted his help.

At the end of 2021, I took a moment to reflect on my life. After spending several Christmas holidays alone due to relationship disappointments, I felt so happy and grateful to have Robert by my side. The right guy had been right in front of me the whole time. All I needed to do was look. I was sure Bernie was jumping for joy. He sent me the perfect man, after all. We got married on June 26, 2024, and are overjoyed.

Walk On By

After my second husband passed away, I decided to explore the world of online dating. The process was simple: I would come home, turn on my computer, and check the dating app to see if anyone had "winked" at me. A wink meant someone had viewed my profile and expressed interest in connecting. One man encouraged me to reach out and arrange a date. The phone conversation went well. He said he would be at a nearby country club the next day, and we could meet there to chat in person. Being new to online dating, I was hesitant to meet him, even in an outdoor setting. Sensing my reluctance, he said, "Listen, I'll drink on the patio near the pool. Why don't you walk by? If you like what you see, feel free to stop and say hello. If not, you can keep walking."

Still nervous, I asked my 87-year-old mother to accompany me. My mom came to America from Poland as a young woman. She still had a strong Eastern European accent and sometimes mispronounced common phrases. For example, she called a blowout at the hair salon as a blowjob. But I digress.

My mother and I drove to the country club, parked, got out, and went to the pool area. We saw a man sitting alone at a table, sipping a drink and reading the newspaper. As we approached, we noticed a substantial horn of calcified epidermis protruding from his head. My mother elbowed me and said, "Sharla, keep walking. You don't need to meet that horny man." We giggled like two young teens, back to the car.

Can't Make This Up

One of the first guys I met on the dating app was Nate. Nate had an interesting backstory. He and his wife lived in a beautiful home in New Jersey in the 1970s. They had two great children, and life was good. That is until his wife of twenty years said she was unhappy and needed to be free. She left him and the kids and never looked back. Nate raised the kids through high school and college before retiring to Florida. He never heard from his wife again.

Nate and I connected right away, but I worried that living with my mother might turn him away. My second husband died around the same time my father did, leaving both my mom and me widows. We pooled our resources and bought a beautiful house together. Even though we sometimes annoyed each other, we were best friends.

It turns out I had nothing to worry about. Nate doted on my mother, proving I had found a good man. When my adult children visited me in Florida, we all went to the movies and out to dinner. My daughter said, "Mom, I like Nate, but he seems too old for you. He's perfect for Grandma." I thought the same thing. Meanwhile, my mother wanted no part of it! Nate and I stopped dating but remained friends.

A month later, Nate received surprising news when his ex-wife contacted him immediately, saying she needed his help. She had been in a severe accident and was facing surgery and a difficult recovery. She asked if she could move in with him and if he would help with her rehabilitation. In return, she promised to split the settlement money once her case was settled, which was a substantial amount. He agreed. Three months later, they remarried and have remained together ever since.

Mal Was Not Nor-Mal

After my husband died, I hoped someone would introduce me to a great guy or that I'd meet Prince Charming on a cruise. That didn't happen, so I turned to online dating. That's how I met Mal, a good-looking, tall, soft-spoken man. After many dates and quality time together, I was curious why Mal never made a move on me. By most people's standards, I'm an attractive, curvy woman. He was a romantic guy. Every morning, I found a beautiful poem in my computer inbox, and he often brought me flowers or chocolates.

Assuming he was too shy to suggest it, I invited him to spend the night. While he washed up, I got into bed, freshly cleaned and wearing a sexy negligee. Mal came out of the bathroom in full-coverage flannel pajamas and lay down on top of the blanket. "Are you going to get under the covers?" I asked. He responded, "No, it's better if I stay out here."

I'm not a nymphomaniac, but I believe intimacy is a vital part of a committed relationship. Mal's firm commitment to a platonic relationship was a dealbreaker for me.

Thank goodness we remained friends. I enjoyed receiving a morning message every day, even though he replaced the poems with silly jokes. When I didn't get an email for three days, I called him. There was no answer. I tried several more times but to no avail. I started to worry and called Mal's son. "This isn't normal for your father. You should go check on him." They had to break down the front door. Mal was lying on the bathroom floor, his head bleeding, inches from death. He lived another five years before passing away from natural causes. I still get a card from Mal's son every Christmas.

Married Lovers

After my husband passed away, I yearned for companionship without commitment. I found myself involved with several married men. Each encounter told a different story: some were on the verge of divorcing or navigating the rough waters of separation, others embraced the complexities of open marriages, and a few wove lies and used deception like skilled artists. No matter their story, without the burden of deep emotional ties, I felt attractive, almost like a goddess.

There's something oddly comforting about married men—they carry a certain domesticated aura, exuding familiarity that puts one at ease. They have an unassuming grace in everyday actions, like carefully putting the toilet seat down, skillfully holding a fork at dinner, or avoiding awkward behaviors in bed.

I deliberately avoided getting involved with men who had young children or whose wives I knew. There was a refreshingly honest quality to these connections. It was clear they were attracted to me, seeking intimacy with someone who could connect with them on both an intellectual and emotional level. They openly sought my company, knowing I wasn't after anything more than our shared moments. In that simplicity, I found exactly what I was looking for.

I felt absolutely no guilt, and to this day, that feeling remains unchanged. The thought of destroying someone else's marriage never crossed my mind; it simply wasn't my intention. One of my married lovers even expressed gratitude, saying our affair had strengthened his relationship. He explained that the secret time away from his daily life allowed him to return home with a renewed spirit, ultimately helping him to live harmoniously with his wife.

My life has gone through a whirlwind of unexpected turns over the past few years, with each twist guiding me down a different path of self-discovery and growth. My involvement with married men is a chapter I often reflect on, a complex web of emotions and experiences that shaped my view on relationships. While it may have worked for me back then, I wouldn't recommend it to others, especially those looking for marriage.

My Condom Conversation

You might find this hard to believe, but I recently had a profound conversation with an unopened condom resting on my nightstand. At fifty-eight years old, I have navigated life without ever using one. My wife and I made a firm commitment to each other right after college, choosing to wait until our wedding night to embrace our intimacy. For thirty-three beautiful years, we shared our lives, creating a bond filled with love and laughter. Tragically, that journey ended when cancer took her from me, leaving me to reflect on memories that now feel bittersweet and lonely.

Almost three years later, I met an incredible woman while playing a lively game of cards at a friend's house. Our connection was immediate, and after a few months of dating filled with laughter and shared memories, we decided it was time to take our relationship to the next level.

As the gentleman I aim to be, I went out and bought a condom in preparation for that special night. In fact, I purchased a three-pack, both optimistic and a bit frightening. After a fifteen-minute standoff with the pharmacy clerk, who kept making direct eye contact, I finally made it home with my purchase.

The chosen one now sat on my nightstand, looking like a tiny, shiny guardian of virtue waiting for its moment to shine. Staring at it with a mix of excitement and sheer panic, I softly muttered, "This will be my first time." In the quiet corners of my imagination, I pictured the condom replying, "Me too, buddy!" With growing anticipation and a slight tremble in my voice, I quipped back, "I can hardly wait!" only to hear that cheeky echo in my mind respond, "Same here!"

We were both in this together, full of hopes and dreams, with a lingering fear that I might put it on backwards and end up having an awkward conversation with my date, the emergency room nurse, and maybe even the local news. Who would have guessed that planning for a big night could involve so much talk with the Trojan horse?

Bobbie's comments:

In the end, whether to date or not to date isn't a question with a universal answer. It's a deeply personal journey that unfolds differently for each of us. Your heart will know when it's ready to welcome new connections, just as it knew how to love before. Remember that the ghost of what was doesn't have to haunt what could be. Dating after loss isn't about replacing what you had; it's about honoring your continued capacity for joy and companionship. Be patient with yourself as you navigate this new territory. Some days, you'll feel ready to conquer the dating world; other days, you'll prefer the company of your favorite slippers and a good book. Both choices are perfectly valid. After all, life is too short to waste on uncomfortable shoes or uncomfortable dates. Whatever path you choose, whether it leads to meaningful new relationships or the rich discovery that you're quite content on your own, approach it with courage, kindness, and the occasional condom conversation when necessary.

Chapter 9 - Cozy Pleasures (Rated R)

Just because you've lost your life partner doesn't mean you've lost all desire for closeness, physical contact, and sexual release. Yes, your lover has gone beyond the veil, but you still exist on this earthly plane, and your needs remain. Along with the desire to connect with others socially, you may also feel a strong urge for more intimate connection. You are grieving, yet your libido still refuses to be ignored.

Everyone grieves in their own way and has different thoughts about appropriate sexual expression after losing a spouse. You might be surprised to discover that, as a sensual person, you've lost your sexual spark. However, this is likely temporary, and as you heal and concentrate on your physical and mental well-being, those familiar needs and desires will come back.

Let's assume, for now, that your sexual desires are acknowledged, but you're not ready to explore them with someone new. Where does that leave you? It leaves the widower with "Rosy Palm and her five sisters!" Joking aside, there is no harm or shame in that. Self-pleasure for men isn't just for adolescent boys with raging hormones. I say, go for it. After all, orgasms relieve stress, dilate blood vessels, and lower blood pressure.

When it comes to self-pleasure, widows, and widowers have a wide array of sex toys, vibrators, gizmos, and gadgets to choose from. Have you ever walked into a

Fascinations store or perused their website? You would be amazed at the variety, assortment, and ingenuity!

According to Lou Paget, a renowned sex educator and author of *Orgasms: How to Have Them, Give Them, and Keep Them Coming*, engaging in self-pleasure enhances your health potential. For one, it boosts levels of dopamine and oxytocin, brain hormones that promote feelings of happiness and well-being. It also increases blood flow to the genital area, making tissues stronger and more resilient. Experiencing orgasms helps strengthen the pelvic floor, reducing the risks of incontinence and vaginal tissue atrophy, while promoting relaxation and improving sleep.

Another benefit of cozy pleasures is their excellent safety record: no unwanted pregnancies, no sexually transmitted diseases, and no need for a partner if you're not ready for one. If you choose to take a lover to bed, you can still engage in your self-care and self-pleasure practices to expand your repertoire.

Caring for your sexual needs is just as important as tending to your body's needs for nutrition, exercise, stress relief, skincare, oral hygiene, or foot care.

Oh, what masturbation can do for your skin! Raising your body temperature dilates the capillaries in your skin, giving you a nice, rosy glow. Beyond the short term, it can slightly increase estrogen levels, helping to prevent collagen breakdown, premature wrinkling, and sagging skin.

Widows Unafraid to Share

- I am a 67-year-old woman who has been single for five years. Many men my age who are dating prefer younger partners or may experience performance issues. I don't feel the need to compete with someone younger, nor do I have the patience for libido challenges. I bought a small, battery-operated gadget that helps me maintain a healthy level of oxytocin, allowing me to sleep soundly through the night. I have no trouble finding my sweet spot.

- I have been single for 16 years, and during this time, I have hesitated to share my secret. It is comforting to find others who also seek sexual satisfaction without intercourse. I keep my secret Johnson toy securely hidden in my dresser drawer.

- I feel sorry for women missing out on personal, cozy pleasures. Whether you seek them with someone or use a gadget makes no difference. What you do with whom is your business if everyone is a consenting adult and nobody gets hurt. Don't overlook your responsibility to care for your body's needs. Your body is your most valuable possession and needs more than just food and water to flourish. The key to improving your personality is satisfying your body's physical needs. I guarantee that pleasuring yourself will make you smile more!

Widow's Fire

While self-pleasure can be beneficial, it may not be enough. Many grieving widows and widowers experience a strong urge to connect sexually with others, a phenomenon known as "widow's fire." This involuntary desire or obsessive need for sex can lead to confusion and distress. For example, after losing a beloved spouse, the physical intimacy you shared can leave a void. Just two weeks later, intense feelings of desire may arise, making it difficult to stop thinking about seeking a sexual connection.

Widow's fire is not solely about the desire for intercourse. It encompasses a longing for connection, physical touch, and the wish to feel desired. One of my friends, Renee, confided in me after her husband of 45 years passed away:

Bobbie, I can't explain how much I missed being touched. Although Arthur and I weren't overly affectionate, we held hands. He rubbed my neck and shoulders when I was tense, and we cuddled in bed. After he passed away, I missed that physical contact. I didn't realize how much until I chose to go through a pat-down at the airport instead of using the scanning machine. The security agent used a firm touch as she moved up each leg to the groin, referring to it as the point of resistance. She then proceeded with sweeping motions under my breasts. I found that the entire 60-second procedure felt delightful and tingly!

Although Renee joked about it, she had to navigate some complicated and confusing feelings of shame and guilt regarding her emotional and physical needs before deciding to find a new partner. Not a replacement for her beloved husband, mind you, but someone new to explore what the world and her body still had to offer.

Craving sex soon after losing a spouse can feel both upsetting and confusing, especially with thoughts like, "What would my children say? What would the neighbors think? Am I a freak?" Research shows that widow's fire is a common way grief shows itself. Whew! It's a relief to know you are not alone in this.

On the other hand, if you notice that you feel sexually shut down and resist the idea of sex, this is simply another way that grief can show up. Everyone experiences it a little differently. Why not be gentle and patient with yourself as you go through your healing process?

Help with Healing

Alison was young, in love, and overflowing with anticipation, hopes, and dreams. When her partner died in a tragic accident, she fell into a profound abyss of grief and loneliness.

For months afterward, Alison struggled to feel empathy and compassion. She didn't want to share her thoughts or connect with anyone. Yet, she needed to experience something more than just a deep emptiness. She needed to feel alive.

The widow's fire struck fiercely! Nearly anything could spark a sudden, uncontrollable urge for sex. Stressful situations were a common trigger. Formal events were challenging. Attending alone, despite being stressful, ignited her with sexual energy and excitement. How utterly confusing.

Alison sought help from a therapist to understand her confusing physical and emotional reactions. She felt relieved to learn they were normal and common, yet she couldn't understand why no one talked about these topics. She reflected, "People die every day all over the world. Are we all walking around feeling unfulfilled and unhealed?"

Not yet ready to date, she turned to masturbation to cope with the deep sense of loss and abandonment.

Therapy, self-reflection, and time helped Alison accept her emotions and physical reactions. She no longer tries to ignore difficult feelings; she embraces them along with the new life she continues to create for herself.

So, You've Decided to Date

Tentatively and excitedly moving forward, you might be surprised to learn that dating after a loss can be a tough challenge. You want to be open and spontaneous, but you also feel the need to protect yourself emotionally, physically, and sexually. You may wonder if you're smart, attractive, or adaptable enough. You might feel self-conscious with someone new compared to how comfortable you felt with your spouse.

When exploring a new sex life, studies show that nearly one-third of widows and widowers believe the benefits outweigh the drawbacks. Engaging in sex can effectively distract from the intense pain of loss. It also releases a burst of feel-good hormones. According to Helen Fisher, PhD, a biological anthropologist, "The body becomes quite broken [after a death], and having decent sex stimulates the dopamine system." This can leave you feeling calm, hopeful, and energized.

For many, the best part is the thrill of trying new things. As much as we would give anything to have our departed lover back, over the years, sex may have shifted from passionate to predictable. There's no need to feel guilty about playful exploration with a considerate new partner.

Dating App for Widows and Widowers

"How am I ever going to find someone to date?" you ask. There are many ways and places to meet new people. You might talk with someone interesting at the supermarket, the gym, a bar, a networking event, a hobby club, or even while on vacation or walking your dog. Someone could introduce you to someone in their social circle who is also looking to date, but don't hold your breath. You might also consider trying online dating.

There are several great dating apps out there, but one recommended to me is *Chapter 2*. This app focuses on widows, widowers, or anyone who has lost a life partner. It was launched in 2022 and created by a widow who had lost her husband two years earlier.

Chapter 2 founders and funders, some of whom are also widowed, realize that many of their users haven't dated in a long time and might be unfamiliar with online dating. The app provides guidance to assist users in taking those hesitant first steps back into the dating scene.

Creating a safe and secure space for people to meet and explore dating again is an excellent idea. Unsurprisingly, Chapter 2 is popular among widows and widowers. It features a comprehensive sign-up process and screens all profiles. App users can report any creepy or suspicious behavior, activities, or messages. Safety remains a top priority!

Besides safety, the Chapter 2 community finds comfort in connecting with others who understand their experiences. The app includes a community forum, a blog, and helpful tips for safe, successful dating. Additionally, it offers in-person events and trips for members. I recommend finding an app or online forum that suits your needs.

My friend Sue does too. After her husband Stan passed away three years ago, a friend gave her a lovely gift: a shiny silver necklace with a long, slim dangling pendant. She immediately liked it, slipped it around her neck, and headed out to meet her adult children for dinner. Seated at the table, her son commented, "Mom, that's an unusual necklace you're wearing. I dare say it looks a bit, um, er... phallic."

Sue gasped, "What are you talking about? Wait, oh my God! Now that I think about it, I believe it came with a computer attachment. That's puzzling. What the heck is this?"

Sue's son unscrewed the top of the pendant to reveal a cable charger's connection point. Then he pressed a discreet button on the side, setting the pendant to vibrate slowly, quickly, or pulse. "Mom, you're wearing a vibrator."

Sue was shocked, embarrassed, and intrigued. She tucked the necklace into her handbag.

Later that evening, she pulled out the sleek, little device. The only vibrators she knew of were big old penis impersonators meant to be inserted. This little gadget was designed for external clitoral stimulation, and it brought on a quick, intense orgasm. Sue was pleased, to say the least.

To Each His or Her Own

Anyone experiencing the excruciating pain of loss should be able to do what makes them feel better, as long as it's not harmful or dangerous. Whether you engage in self-pleasure, find a lover, or both—whatever works for you. If you decide to explore sex with a new partner, I recommend avoiding comparisons with other widows or widowers. When it comes to sex after loss, only you can determine what is right for you and when.

Chapter 10 - Other Fun Things To Do

What talents lie dormant within you? It might be time to set up that paint easel, dust off those piano keys, write that memoir, or sign up for tennis or pickleball lessons. While we're at it, which groups might share interests like yours? A hiking group? Birdwatching? Ham radio? The possibilities are endless. If nothing comes to mind, here are some suggestions.

Classes

- Acting class

- Art classes, calligraphy, painting

- Arts and crafts

- Astrology, tarot cards, palm reading

- Baking, cake decorating

- Car restoration

- Cooking

- Comedy, improv classes, stand-up

- Community college classes

- Dance lessons

- Flower arranging

- Glass engraving

- Jewelry making

- Knitting, crocheting, needlepoint, beading, quilting, weaving

- Foreign language lessons

- Pottery

- Mahjong

- Martial arts, Tai Chi

- Meditation

- Metalworking class

- Musical instrument, singing lessons, musical bands

- Photography

- Podcasting

- Scrapbooking

- Sculpting

- Sewing

- Welding

- Winemaking or beer-brewing

- Woodworking, furniture refinishing

- Writing, poetry

- Yoga, Pilates, kickboxing, stretch classes

Groups/Clubs/Organizations

- Book clubs

- Board games

- Camping or glamping

- Car clubs

- Card game clubs: Bridge, Pinochle, Gin Rummy, or Poker

- Chess clubs

- Choirs

- Community theater organizations

- Writers' groups

- Dancing clubs

- Film enthusiast clubs

- Fitness clubs

- Gardening clubs

- Genealogy

- National Park Travelers Club

- Outdoor adventure groups

- Parenting groups

- Pet ownership, training, socializing organizations

- Religious congregations, Bible studies

- Seniors' groups

- Social clubs

- Travel clubs

- Veteran organizations

- Writers' groups

- Lion taming (I just wanted to see if you were still paying attention!)

Sports/Hobbies
- Aquatics

- Archery

- Boating

- Bowling

- Coaching

- Cricket

- Cycling

- Fishing

- Gardening

- Golfing

- Hiking

- Hockey

- Ice or roller skating

- Indoor rock climbing

- Kayaking

- Metal detecting

- Pickleball, Tennis

- Pool, Billiards

- Racquetball

- Sailing

- Snowboarding

- Surfing

- Vehicle restoration

- Video production

- Volleyball

Volunteer positions:
- Performing arts centers, book festivals, library docent programs, historical society programs, senior centers, food banks, Meals on Wheels, The American Red Cross, Humane Society, Salvation Army, Desert Botanical Gardens, Parks & Recreation, VITA tax assistance, airports, committee and board member opportunities, tour guide, philanthropic

organizations, reading to children, reading to the elderly, pet fostering

Tip: It's always fun to volunteer at local live community theaters so that you can see the performance for free! Ushers are responsible for welcoming patrons, collecting tickets, and assisting them in finding their seats.

- Amateur Cold Case Investigation/Volunteer: The Cold Case Foundation is devoted to raising public awareness and creating partnerships to assist law enforcement and provide them with the resources needed to bring closure.

- https://www.coldcasefoundation.org/

- https://ncjtc.fvtc.edu/training/details

Side Jobs

- Bookkeeping

- House sitting

- Pet sitting

- Rideshare driver

- Tutoring

- Pet care services

- Survey or focus groups

I included these lists because I believe staying active and engaged in life is very important. Being bored for too long can make you feel dull. According to *Columbia News*, published by Columbia University: "Chronic boredom is associated with impulsivity and risky behavior, including careless driving, compulsive gambling, drug and alcohol abuse, reckless thrill-seeking, and other self-destructive behaviors. People who are bored easily are susceptible to depression, anxiety, anger, academic failure, poor work performance, loneliness, and isolation."

Not ready to venture out yet? New fitness apps and virtual classes are making it easier than ever to stay fit from home. Whether you're into yoga or dancing, there's something for everyone.

Exploring new activities or rekindling old passions, pastimes, and interests can give you direction and a renewed sense of purpose. Connecting with others can lift you from the doldrums and brighten your spirit. Engaging in enjoyable activities brings you joy, and when you experience joy, you can share it with others.

I know you want to be a bright light in the world, but you might need to push yourself a little, at least at first. I bet you can come up with a few ideas I hadn't considered, and once you're involved in something rewarding and fun, I'd love to hear what inspired you to get off the couch.

Chapter 11 - Bits and Pieces

It's comforting to say that time heals all wounds, but I've learned that the real challenge is how long we allow ourselves to stay stuck in pain. We have a choice: we can drown in self-pity or take small steps toward reclaiming our lives. Finding activities that bring us joy and help us grow can light the way to a brighter future. I believe in only giving advice when someone asks for it. But this time, I'm making an exception. I'm sharing these suggestions based on my own experiences and the wisdom of caring friends and professionals who have helped me see new ways to navigate the healing journey.

Walking it out

- If you are feeling frustration, regret, or even anger, walking can help you burn off those emotions. When we feel difficult emotions, cortisol, and epinephrine (adrenalin) course through our bloodstream, elevating blood pressure. It can take several days for the body to break down and eliminate these hormones. Science shows that exercise rids our bodies of excess stress hormones. Endorphins, chemicals our bodies produce while exercising, can help relieve stress and pain and restore a sense of well-being.

- During the acute stages of grief, I found it was not enjoyable to watch movies on television anymore, at least until I got used to watching them alone. Eating felt impossible, so I had to push myself to consume smaller meals to ensure I had enough energy to get through the day. Socializing was completely out of the question, but walking helped energize my body and provided the space to process my thoughts. If you walk on a nature trail, take long, circular hikes; you'll notice more beauty each time around. Develop an awareness of the magic happening all around us at any given moment.

Find some wheels

- Consider the healing power of a road trip. You may be surprised at how relaxing it is to travel alone or with a friend. Driving through open spaces allows you to process your thoughts and emotions, leading to personal growth and clarity. For me personally, experiencing new places reduces stress and enhances mental health. Just make sure the trip is enjoyable. Pack a cooler with water and snacks, stop for restroom breaks, and enjoy a fun lunch. Don't forget to take photos of nature's beauty along the way.

- Cycling is a popular sport. If you prefer not to ride solo, there are numerous clubs you can join, or you can ask a friend. Also, you can investigate indoor bicycling classes called spin sessions. They're a great form of exercise until you feel ready to take on a bike ride outside. Remember the old saying, "Four wheels move the body, two wheels move the soul.

Little things that make a surprising difference

- Music has a profound impact on our emotions and overall well-being. Take a moment to curate a playlist filled with songs that evoke cherished memories from different stages of your life. Whether it's a special summer, an unforgettable road trip, or simply tunes from your youth, listening to these tracks can evoke happiness and a sense of connection to your past. Consider dancing or singing along as you engage in music that stimulates both your body and mind, making it a delightful way to boost your mood! Enjoying your favorite music daily is beneficial. Studies have demonstrated that music can alleviate pain, enhance memory, and strengthen the delicate pathways in the brain. I lean towards smooth jazz, but I also appreciate oldies and country music from time to time.

- Books are therapeutic. Keep one close and read it before bedtime or listen to a story on Audible. Thought-provoking stories transport you to different places and times, bringing joy and mental stimulation. When I can't sleep because my mind refuses to shut down, I move to a comfy chair and read a book (not a mobile device, an actual book) using a soft light. When I feel tired, I go back to bed and focus on the characters instead of my personal thoughts. It usually works.

- Writing can be invigorating. I began writing during the pandemic when we felt like prisoners in our own homes. I joined an online writing group that helped me start this book you are reading now. We provided critiques of each other's work, which was helpful. You could start jotting down notes for your own memoir or let your imagination run wild.

Allow yourself some fun time

•When I crave chocolate, I opt for dark chocolate in moderation.

•I firmly believe laughter is good for the soul and essential for overall well-being. Life might give us a lot to feel stressed or miserable about, but if you can find ways to keep laughter in your day, you can live a longer, healthier life. Any laughs will do when you're blue, whether that's a chat with a friend, your favorite television comedy, or silly pet videos on the internet.

- Think about the possibility of welcoming a furry companion into your life. Dog and cat owners tend to be more physically active and less susceptible to stress. Their companionship fosters a comforting presence in your home but also fills a gap in your heart.

Write it down

- A gratitude list is helpful, even though being grateful while grieving isn't easy. At the top of the list, consider adding simple things we often take for granted, like the sun rising each day or enjoying the beautiful sunsets every evening. Acknowledge your body for taking you from place to place and include the food on your table and the safety of your living environment. Then, recognize those who have stood by you or a pet offering endless love during this sensitive time. Watch your gratitude list grow as the days pass. Don't forget to include those who brighten your day with kind words or a warm smile.

Find ways to stay occupied

- Hobbies are another way to stay busy. Painting, photography, and gardening can take your mind off your emotions. Growing vegetables throughout the seasons will keep you busy. If one hobby doesn't work for you, don't give up. As you saw in the last chapter, there are many options to choose from.

- Keep your mind energized by reading, journaling, or playing an instrument or a challenging game. Many games are available online, including sudoku, crossword puzzles, mah jong, and word games like Dropwords and Word Connect. Google them!

- For those who haven't worked outside the home in a while, discovering that part-time work offers structure, social interaction, and a sense of purpose can be enlightening. Whether consulting in your previous field, working at a local garden center, or teaching at a community center, these positions can help you stay mentally sharp and keep your mind engaged and away from depression.

Healthy suggestions

- If you are experiencing sleepless nights, avoid drinking products with caffeine after 2:00 pm. Give tea a try. Chamomile is a soothing herbal tea. Chamomile and other calming herbal tea blends can help quiet your mind, allowing you to drift off to a better night's sleep. Certain foods can disrupt sleep. Avoid eating aged cheese, popcorn, citrus fruits, and tomatoes or consuming coffee, cocoa, or alcohol before bedtime.

- I use a standing desk. It has improved my posture, and I get fewer leg cramps.

- I understand it may be difficult to stay emotionally strong after the loss of a loved one. Alcohol and drugs may provide temporary relief, but they are a crutch that can cloud the reality we're trying to come to terms with. I hope you muster the strength to avoid temptations that sabotage your well-being and lead to bad decisions. Remember, you are the only one in charge of your mind and body. Don't let alcohol or drugs influence your decision-making as you navigate through these changes. More-than-moderate alcohol consumption (generally, more than one drink a day for women or more than two a day for men) leads to a shorter life span. You could lose your job, friends, and, most importantly, your health. Every one of us has a choice as to how we want to live our lives. I prefer to be in control of mine, and I think you do too. Stay strong, dear one. Just say: "No, I'd prefer to have water."

Acceptance

- The life we had before is no longer an option. We must accept the fact that change is at hand. Change is healthy and vital, but it can also be frightening. Marriages are brief or long, healthy or dysfunctional, and death comes suddenly or slowly over the years. We all experience the journey through grief differently. Be open to your new life and accept it with courage and perseverance.

Reminders

- Should a woman keep her husband's name after his death or even after a divorce? I mentioned this in Chapter 7, but it bears repeating. It's a personal choice, not a requirement. You have the right to choose your own identity. I encourage you to embrace your individuality and make choices that empower you.

- Take time before making big decisions. After losing a loved one, our emotional brains can supersede our rational minds. As I've said, making significant changes too soon could be a mistake we regret later. Please consider talking to a professional or a loved one before you sign that document or check!

- Acts of kindness can help heal your heart. When you are feeling down, consider helping others in need. You never know if they are suffering or how deeply. Assisting someone less fortunate than you can provide a much-needed sense of purpose when you feel tossed about by the winds of grief. Take another look at the volunteer opportunities in Chapter 10.

Senior Home Safety: Quick Guide

- Create a safe home environment

- Keep walkways clear and well-lit, both inside and outside

- Secure loose rugs to prevent tripping

- Install grab bars and non-slip mats in bathrooms

- Use motion-activated or remote-controlled lighting

- Get a Medical Alert System

Choose one with 24/7 monitoring and fall detection. MGHome Cellular uses 4G LTE (no landline needed). Works up to 1,400 feet from home and includes waterproof buttons for shower safety.

- Install a lockbox

Provides emergency access to your home. Share the code only with trusted people. It's essential if you fall and can't answer the door.

Helps emergency responders, family, and friends access your home when needed.

Wisdom From Others

Annie Growth is a certified professional coach and popular speaker, and founder of Pearls of Wisdom AZ. She offered two compelling pieces of advice for when your loved one is still alive:

- "Record voices while you can. As you know, we often forget the sound of people's laughter and their voices over time. My dad, both of my moms, and my grandma passed away before we carried recording devices in our pockets. I would give anything to hear their voices and laughter just one more time. I remember moments, like one with my stepmom, where we laughed so hard we cried, and my face hurt. I try to hear that laughter again in my mind, but it never quite comes back."

- "Take pictures often, and keep them as current as you can. I don't have any photos of my loved ones from their last ten years of life. Now, with a cell phone camera always in hand, make sure to use it. And don't forget to take a few selfies with them."

I'd like to add to Annie's advice. Consider creating a "life story video." You can put one together on your own or contact a professional company that will preserve your memories and provide a legacy. This is another way for you to be able to keep hearing their voice.

Harriet Cabelly, a clinical social worker, author, and positive psychology coach, also shared some inspirational thoughts that resonated with me. I hope they touch your heart as well:

- "When a loved one dies, we carry our grief with us forever. Their missing piece does not get filled in. Instead, we grow around the emptiness, expanding our lives with renewed purpose and meaning."

- "Being aware of our own mortality imbues our life with intention. It's like the little birdie on our shoulder, keeping us on our toes of conscious living: living into what matters to us, what we value, and stepping into ourselves with greater awareness and excitement. We take and give with fierceness and urgency, not knowing when our time is up."

- "Norman Cousins, author of the bestseller *Anatomy of an Illness,* said, 'Death is not the greatest loss in life. The greatest loss is what dies inside us while we live.

'Don't let any part of yourself die while you are alive. Step into your fabulous self. Work on healing the rough patches. Take pride in your self-work. This is where we transcend our circumstances and begin to feel joy from the inside out.

'Create your own modern traditions — As life changes, we often find ourselves caught in routines or patterns. Embrace the chance to establish new traditions that align with your current lifestyle, whether a monthly potluck with friends, a bi-weekly book club, or a seasonally themed gathering. These rituals can enhance your sense of community and create joyful moments to anticipate, reinforcing vital social connections for longevity.'"

Janet Gourand, founder of Tribe Sober, writer, podcaster, and recovery coach, speaks from experience: "Did you know that the average dependent drinker will struggle alone for about 11 years before reaching out for help? Don't let alcohol or drugs influence your decision-making as you navigate these changes in your life."

Here are some wise words from the actor Jim Carrey:
- "Grief is not just an emotion—it's an unraveling, a space where something once lived but is now gone. It carves through you, leaving a hollow ache where love once resided.

"In the beginning, it feels unbearable, like a wound that will never close. But over time, the raw edges begin to mend. The pain softens, but the imprint remains—a quiet reminder of what once was. The truth is, you never truly 'move on.' You move with it. The love you had does not disappear; it transforms. It lingers in the echoes of laughter, in the warmth of old memories, in the silent moments where you still reach for what is no longer there. And that's okay.

"Grief is not a burden to be hidden. It is not a weakness to be ashamed of. It is the deepest proof that love existed, that something beautiful once touched your life. So let yourself feel it. Let yourself mourn. Let yourself remember.

"There is no timeline, no 'right' way to grieve. Some days will be heavy, and some will feel lighter. Some moments will bring unexpected waves of sadness, while others will fill you with gratitude for the love you were lucky enough to experience.

"Honor your grief, for it is sacred. It is a testament to the depth of your heart. And in time, through the pain, you will find healing—not because you have forgotten, but because you have learned how to carry both love and loss together."

Two more wonderful quotes for you about helping others:

- **From Raven Wilson**, an extraordinary special event coordinator in the Phoenix, Arizona area: "Never stop being a good person; just change who gets your kindness."

Dr Brenda Combs, EDD

Where You Are is Not Where You'll Stay

You don't need to be perfect; you just need to be present.

Healing isn't about pretending to have it all together. It's about learning how to stay when everything in you used to run. It's about showing up on your hard days, not just your good ones. That's where the real growth happens.

You are building a new life, not fixing an old one. So stop looking back.

You're not that person anymore.

Breathe. Trust the process. Stay in the fight.

You're not alone, and you're not done yet.

- **Katherine Hepburn**, the Oscar-winning actress known for her blunt, feisty personality, said: "When you are feeling sad, do something for someone else."

Your Second Life Begins

Confucius said that everyone has two lives, and the second begins when they realize they only have one. I've adapted Confucius's quote to fit our situation: You only get one life, but when your spouse passes away, you start living a second one.

- The Threshold Between Lives

When we lose the person who shared our days, our dreams, and our deepest moments, it can feel like the world has ended. In many ways, it has—the world you knew, the life you built together, the future you planned. That ending is real, and your grief honors what was sacred.

But within that ending lies a profound truth: you are still here. Still breathing. Still capable of love, growth, and meaning. This isn't about moving on from your spouse or forgetting what you shared. It's about learning to carry their love forward while discovering who you are now, in this changed landscape of your heart.

- The Door That Awaits

Think of this transition not as abandoning your first life, but as standing before a door that has quietly appeared. Behind you lies a room filled with precious memories, shared laughter, and a love that death cannot diminish.

That room will always be part of your home—you can visit it whenever you need to feel close to what you've lost.

The door before you doesn't ask you to leave those memories behind. Instead, it invites you to bring the best of what you learned, the strength you discovered, and the love you shared into spaces yet unexplored. This door opens not to escape your grief, but to find new ways to honor both your loss and your continued presence in this world.

- The Courage to Begin Again

Change requires intention, but intention requires gentleness with yourself. Your second life won't look like anyone else's, and it doesn't need to. Some days, opening that door might mean:

Rediscovering your own rhythms: What do you enjoy when the day is entirely yours to shape? What brings you peace? What sparks curiosity?

Nurturing connections: Reaching out to friends who knew you both, and also cultivating new friendships with people who know you as you are now can keep you moving.

Exploring postponed dreams: Perhaps there were interests, travels, or pursuits that took a backseat during your partnership. These can become threads in the fabric of your second life.

Creating new traditions: Find ways to honor your spouse's memory while building practices that sustain you—whether that's a daily walk, volunteering for a cause they cared about, or simply allowing yourself to find joy again.

- Permission to Live Fully

Your second life isn't a betrayal of your first. It's a testament to the love you shared and the person you became through that partnership. Your spouse, who loved you deeply, would want you to find meaning, connection, and even happiness again. They would want you to use the strength they helped you discover.

This doesn't mean the sadness disappears or that you'll stop missing them. It means you learn to carry your love for them alongside your love for life itself. You learn that grief and gratitude can coexist, that memory and hope can walk hand in hand.

- Moving Forward, Not Moving On

As you step into your second life, remember:

You're not leaving your spouse behind; you're taking the best of what they gave you into new territory. Their influence, their love, the person you became through knowing them, all of this travels with you.

There's no timeline for this transition. Some people feel ready to explore their second life months after their loss. Others need years. Both paths are valid. Trust your own readiness.

Your second life can honor your first. The values you shared, the lessons you learned together, and the way they loved you become guideposts as you navigate new terrain.

The door to your second life stands patiently waiting. It will wait until you're ready. When that time comes—and you'll know when it does—you can step through carrying everything that matters: their memory, their love, and the beautiful truth that you are still here, still capable of creating meaning, still deserving of a life well-lived.

Your second life begins not when you forget your first, but when you choose to let love continue in new forms.

Bobbie's Wish

May you understand that grief and joy can co-exist. Permit yourself to laugh when something strikes you as funny, to be awed by the beauty of nature, and to be open to the joy surrounding you. There is no guilt or shame in finding joy. Doing so does not diminish or dishonor the memory of your loved one. On the contrary, your loved one's spirit is set free when you allow joy back into your heart.

Acknowledgments

When I started writing about my journey through widowhood, I never expected how many hands and hearts would help shape this book. Every person mentioned here has played a vital role in turning my personal experience into something I hope will inspire others facing similar challenges.

To those who bravely shared their stories in the "Voices From the Ones Left Behind" and "To Date or Not to Date" chapters, your honest reflections add authenticity and a variety of perspectives to these pages. Your courage in revealing your vulnerabilities has woven a tapestry of shared experiences that will comfort and guide others.

My editor, Dr. Alisa Cooper, skillfully transformed my scattered thoughts into the compassionate message I envisioned. She enhanced my relatability and communication with my readers by giving voice to my feelings.

Barbara Youngs meticulous copy editing highlighted the depth of my story in ways I couldn't have imagined.

Lilian Suzette Salcido brought my vision to life with her thoughtfully designed butterfly life cycle illustration, which beautifully reflects the journey through widowhood. I am proud to have her as part of my extended family.

Linda Pressman's Life Stories virtual classes through The Scottsdale Arts helped me uncover the story inside my story. Linda, along with my fellow students, helped me bring my vision to life.

Christina Engle with Photo Fusion Studio in Phoenix, Arizona, captured the front cover photo and the back cover headshot.

The Scottsdale Society of Women Writers and critique group members Patricia Brooks, Darlene Ziebell, and Dr. Rose Garlasco offered diverse perspectives and continuous motivation.

Bing and Carol Brown introduced me to the Rim Country Chapter of the Arizona Professional Writers and encouraged me to share my story. Sadly, they both passed away before I could finish it. Connie Cockrell and Marie Fasano continued to support my education within the APW network.

I'm thankful to Carol Baxter for her insights on menu design.

A heartfelt thank you to my dear friends Didi Aldine Davis, Trudy Wells-Meyers, and Steve Danish for proofreading and encouraging me to share my experiences.

My cousin Jeanna Kay Livvix provided family research that gave me clarity and peace.

Kyle Richardson, my financial advisor, went above and beyond during my most vulnerable moments, giving me the peace of mind to focus on healing and writing.

"Tony Vicich, Anders Berg, and Keith Ellis – three incredible comedians who took my humor from ordinary to stage ready. Thank you!"

Finally, I would like to express my deepest gratitude to my family, whose unwavering support throughout this healing process made this book possible. Your patience, understanding, and encouragement carried me through this journey.

This book captures not only my journey through widowhood but also the collective wisdom of many who have traveled similar paths. I hope it provides both comfort and guidance for those starting their next chapter.

End Notes

Writing Groups & Affiliates

Arizona Professional Writers (APW) formerly Arizona Press Women www.arizonaprofessionalwriters.org

Arizona Authors Association (AAA) www.arizonaauthors.org

Phoenix Writers Club (PWC) www.phoenixwritersclub.com

National Federation of Press Women (NFPW) www.nfpw.org/

Scottsdale Society of Women Writers (SSWW) www.brooksgoldmannpublishing.com

Dr. Alisa Cooper, Author, Editor, Book Coach www.thewriterehab.com

Barbara A Youngs, Editor; Retired Coordinator, Honors Writing Center at Northern Arizona University

Carol Baxter, Author, Editor, Book Shepherd, www.talesofatime.net

Cindi Reiss, President, PWC, www.phoenixwritersclub.com

Connie Cockrell, Published Author, APW Past President www.conniesrandomthoughts.com

Darlene Ziebell, Business Consultant, Author, Public Speaker, www.darleneziebell.com

Don McCauley, marketing/publicity strategist www.freepublicitygroup.com

Linda Pressman, Author, Editor, Instructor, Writing Coach, www.lindajpressman.com

Marie Fasano, Published Author, Freelance Writer, Pilot, Registered Nurse

Patricia Brooks, Published Author, Speaker, President/Founder, Scottsdale Society of Women Writers www.brooksgoldmannpublishing.com

Rose Garlasco, PhD, Published Author

Steve Danish, Published Author, One Soldier's Memories

Trudy Wells-Meyers, Author, Award Winning Hair Designer, www.trudywells-meyer.com

Social Networking Groups

Annie Groth, Coach, Founder/Pearls of Wisdom AZ. www.anniegrothyouknowbest.com

eWomen Network

Sandra Yancey, Founder and CEO, www.ewomennetwork.com

Veronica Balm, Executive Managing Director, Phoenix/Scottsdale AZ, www.veronicabahn.com

Raven, Marketing/Production/Management/Hosting www.ravenevents.com

Sue Barenholtz, Founder and Queen of Wild Boomer Women

Comedy & Showbiz

Amanda Melby, Actor-Training Boutique Studio – www.vervestudio.net

Anders Berg, Laughter Matters, Ahwatukee Comedy Club Facilitator

Tony Vicich, Comedian, Owner/Instructor www.comedyschools.com

Keith Ellis, Comedian/actor, www.keithelliscomedy.weebly.com

Dr. Brenda Combs, Writer/Author/Creative Director of Finding My Shoes Foundation and BRC Theatre Group www.brendacombs.com

Ken Clemmer, Back Porch Bandits www.reverbnation.com/kenclemmer.thebackporchbandits

Three Wedding Rings Part One

Rita Davenport, Hall of Fame Keynote Speaker, Author, Radio Broadcaster, Producer/ Host of her own television show. www.ritadavenport.com

Taking Care of Business

Kyle Richardson, CFP, Founding Partner, Financial Advisor, www.waterma
rkwealthteam.com/resource-center/estate

https://www.archives.gov/veterans/military-service-records

One Plate, One Fork

Mary Lee, Grief Coach www.widowlution.com/eating-out-along-while-wid
owed

Marston's San Pasqual dressing (Bobbie recommends) www.marstonproduc
ts.com

Carolyn Golden www.aworkinprocess.us

Voices From the Ones Left Behind

Carey Conley, Author, Speaker, Vision Leader www.careyconley.com

Janet Youngs Norwood, Jan's Happy Place, blogs

Jody Sharpe, Published Author, www.jodysharpe.com

Kebba Buckley Button, MC, OM, Healing Therapeutics www.kebba.com

Laraine (Lari) Yasui, www.facebook.com/lariy

Stephan Wu, www.facebook.com/stephenywu66

Tonya Griffin, Actress

Valorie Newman, Recording Artist www.valorie-spellbound.com

Victoria Benoit, Healer, Coach, Speaker, Author www.extraordinaryoutcom
espublishing.com

To Date or Not to Date

https://www.prevention.com/sex/relationships/g26519484/over-50-dating-a
dvice/

https://www.momjunction.com/articles/dating-after-60_00716144/

https://www.themanual.com/culture/modern-relationship-terms-explained/
#dt/-heading-haunting

Cozy Pleasures

https://www.thewidowshandbook.com/home/widows-fire

https://www.vice.com/en/article/8xwd5v/grief-can-make-you-horny/

https://widowsfire.co.uk/

https://helenfisher.com/

Other Fun Things to Do

https://helpfulprofessor.com/social-groups-examples/

https://simple.wikipedia.org/wiki/List_of_hobbies

https://coldcaseinc.com/how-amateur-sleuths-are-solving-unsolved-case-files

Bobbie's Bits & Pieces

Harriet Cabelly, Clinical Social Worker, Author, Positive Psychology Coach www.rebuildlifenow.com

Janet Gourand, Writer, Podcaster, Recovery Coach, Founder www.tribesober.com

Dr. Brenda Combs, Writer/Author/Creative Director of Finding My Shoes Foundation and BRC Theatre Group, www.brendacombs.com

Annie Groth, Coach, Founder/Pearls of Wisdom AZ. www.anniegrothyouknowbest.com

Raven, Marketing/Production/Management/Hosting, www.ravenevents.com

About the Author

I was born in 1946 in Chicago, but don't let that city-slicker beginning fool you. My real-life lessons came from a humble rural farm in West Union, Illinois, where my grandparents raised my younger brother and me after my parents' divorce. There, I learned to swim in the muddy waters of the Wabash River, encountered chiggers for the first time, and developed a lifelong craving for beefsteak tomatoes picked fresh off the vine.

The family bathroom was an outhouse where one could read the Sears, Roebuck catalog before tearing out a page for its important secondary use. Our water was pumped from an outdoor well and heated on the stove for cooking, cleaning, and the much-needed Saturday night bath. Grandma always let me take the first bath before anyone else. Little did I know that these rustic country roots would give me the grit and humor necessary for the colorful journey that lay ahead.

My teenage years were spent in Chicago, where my younger brother and I squeezed into a three-room apartment behind our mom's tavern. Every night, the twangy sounds of George Jones and Loretta Lynn blasted from the jukebox until the wee hours, but honestly, we couldn't have cared less about the noise. We were just over the moon to be a family again. After school, I took the city bus to American Bandstand every day. Dancing was my whole world, and nobody batted an eye when I landed a job as a GoGo dancer.

By 1971, I had moved to Scottsdale, Arizona, with husband number one. Since then, I have collected three marriage certificates, two death certificates, and one divorce decree—a paper trail that has taught me more about resilience than any self-help book could. I often tell the members of my 'Starting Over... Again' workshop, "If you can't be a good example, at least be a colorful one."

When summers in Phoenix become unbearably hot, I drive to my cabin in the pines north of Payson. There, I write and edit the monthly newsletter for Beaver Valley Estates. My writing skills were recognized in 2024 when the National Federation of Press Women awarded me first place in the Arizona contest and second place nationally for outstanding online newsletter publications.

When I'm not writing, you might find me performing in community theater around town, where I portray eccentric elderly women long before I became one. My face has appeared in local television commercials, enthusiastically endorsing everything from heating and cooling companies to luxury retirement communities. I even tried my hand at stand-up comedy, discovering that my life stories generate much more laughter when shared on stage than when told to a therapist.

But my most cherished role is being a grandma to my lively and wonderful grandchildren. I host "Grandma's Day" outings for each grandchild, which feature one-on-one activities tailored to their interests. Every December, I put together a Grandma's Day Yearbook filled with photos and their candid comments about everything from my yellow teeth to my cooking lessons ("dessert first"). These books preserve my legacy by capturing precious moments in time that might otherwise be lost.

Through three marriages, career changes, and countless planned and unplanned adventures, I have mastered the art of transforming everyday moments into unforgettable stories.

My simple life philosophy is to collect experiences instead of regrets, to laugh, especially when things go wrong, and to always carry a spare change of underwear in case nature elevates laughter to a whole new level.

www.ingramcontent.com/pod-product-compliance
Lightning Source LLC
Chambersburg PA
CBHW070916130626
46555CB00001B/155